THE COMPLETE GUIDE TO
SAILING & SEAMANSHIP

THE COMPLETE GUIDE TO SAILING & SEAMANSHIP

Twain Braden

Illustrations by
Sam Manning

Skyhorse Publishing

Skyhorse Publishing books may be purchased in bulk at special discounts for sales promotion, corporate gifts, fund-raising, or educational purposes. Special editions can also be created to specifications. For details, contact the Special Sales Department, Skyhorse Publishing, 307 West 36th Street, 11th Floor, New York, NY 10018 or info@skyhorsepublishing.com.

Skyhorse® and Skyhorse Publishing® are registered trademarks of Skyhorse Publishing, Inc.®, a Delaware corporation. www.skyhorsepublishing.com

10 9 8 7 6 5 4 3 2 1

Library of Congress Cataloging-in-Publication Data is available on file

ISBN: 978-1-61608-246-8

Printed in China

TABLE OF CONTENTS

This book is dedicated to the memory
of my father, Tom Braden,
not much of a sailor but a hell of a guy.
—*TB*

INTRODUCTION

The stories and examples detailed here take place on a boat that does not exist. Rather, its design was hatched by Sam Manning and me to best illustrate the approach to sailing that we offer in this book. This hypothetical boat is a twenty-foot, full-keel sloop with a jib and mainsail. The vessel has an inboard diesel engine. The hull construction doesn't matter for our purposes, but I often discuss (and Sam has drawn) a boat made of wood because of the universality of the parts of a boat made of wood, such as the frames, stem, transom, and planking. The scenes that these terms illustrate are easily translated to a boat with a fiberglass hull. And while many of the drawings show a gaff rig—largely because of partiality on our part having to do with its attractiveness and joy of handling—the same principles of boat handling apply to a Marconi-rigged boat. We will call it *Swallow*, for reasons explained below.

The approach I take to learning to sail and to becoming expert in handling a small boat at sea represents a certain philosophy—an amalgamation of my own and that of countless others I've sailed with over the years. This is not the only way to learn to sail. It's simply one way of many by which a novice can approach sailing. But it's one gleaned from years of experience teaching people, not so much how to sail as much as how to handle a boat under sail. There's a big difference. Sailing itself is simply the mechanics of how a boat works under sail. *Handling* a boat under sail, however, is about seamanship itself, from the rigging to the hull; from the dock to the island; and from the anchorage home again—and everything in between.

This is not a comprehensive treatise on sailing. It's a purposefully slim volume that is intended to be accessible to the lay reader who simply wants an approximation of the concepts of sailing—roughly 90 percent of what you need to know to get started. The subject is simply too vast and is available elsewhere in more specific books—whether on navigation, anchoring, or rough-weather boat handling. The other elements of sailing,

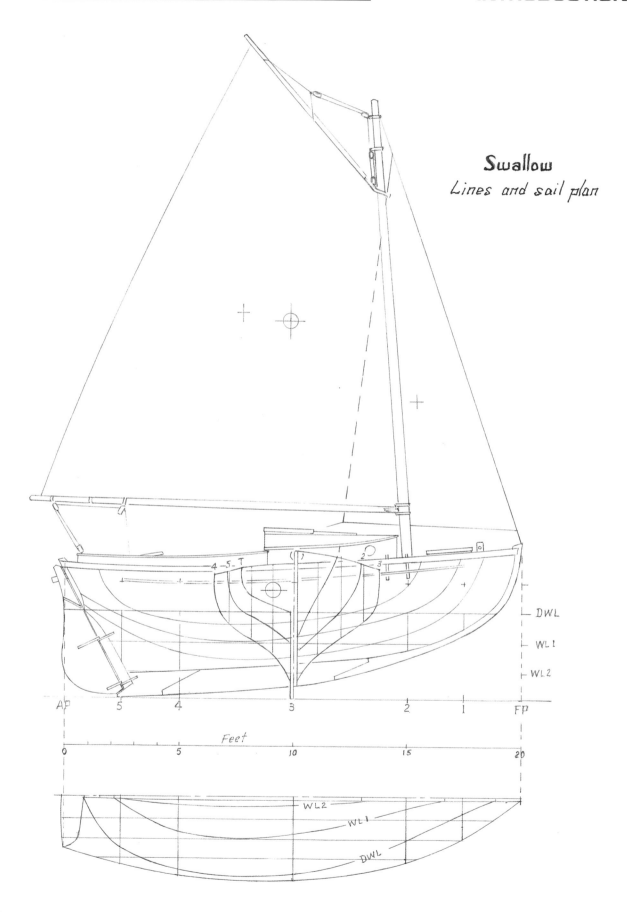

Swallow
Lines and sail plan

Swallow under sail

which are really the greatest parts, will be acquired through experience. A little background knowledge is helpful, of course, but really there's nothing more valuable and enjoyable than jumping into a small boat, getting underway, and learning (carefully!) as you go.

Some time ago I went sailing with Scottish adventurer Sir Chay Blyth in Boston's outer harbor. As a magazine editor at the time, I was invited with other media types to experience his nimble vessels, the fleet that he used for his so-called Challenge Business, so that we might be charmed enough by their handling that we would be inclined to write favorably about them. The boats were fine enough, about seventy feet overall, and proved fast and sturdy as their young, professional Australo-British crew put them through their paces in the summer breezes. But what was most interesting to me was the story Sir Chay told me as we tacked our way eastward out of the harbor while standing on the foredeck.

Sir Chay is a small man, about five-and-a-half feet tall, but his stature grew with his energy as the story unfolded, until he seemed a giant as he waved his arms emphatically, his Scottish brogue punctuating each salient point with the air of an ancient Highland giant.

He told me that when he had set about planning to build a fleet of boats to sail around the world with paying passengers, he hired his long-time designer friend Andrew Roberts. He asked Roberts to come up with a concept for a vessel that would maximize sea-kindliness and accommodate a sizeable number of paying passengers so that voyages could generate a profit, but be inexpensive enough to build because they needed no customization. In short, every part should be off-the-shelf to minimize cost yet be assembled in such a way as to maximize overall size so that the largest number of paying passengers could be accommodated.

He asked me:

"If you were to build such a fleet of vessels that were to carry passengers around the world on a yacht race, where would you start? How big would the boat be? How many passengers?"

"I don't know," I mumbled vaguely, "perhaps for a crew of ten? Start with ten berths?" It seemed like a nice even number.

"Why ten?" he asked. "Why not eleven—or nine?"

I had no answer. And he smiled rather like he knew the joke was on me.

He then described how this question had plagued him and the designer for months. They needed some benchmark that would dictate the starting point and therefore the rest of the design. In this country, people wanting to sail boats for profit have such a benchmark. Six passengers are all you can carry if you don't want the Coast Guard spending too much time asking questions about safety gear. You can have an "uninspected passenger vessel" carry six paying passengers, and they'll leave you alone so long as you provide lifejackets for all. As a result, many low-budget commercial outfits choose this number to design their business around. The number six dictates the highest number of berths (plus one or two crew), which dictates the overall size of the boat. One much smaller and you can't maximize profit; one much larger and you're wasting money. But there are no such restrictions in other countries, and, besides, Blyth was aiming higher than the U.S. Coast Guard's standards anyway.

Finally, Blyth received a call from Roberts in the middle of the night. The designer was in a fit of passion, in the throes of a kind of Archimedes'-eureka-by-Jove euphoria, that would yield the key to how to proceed with the design.

"It was the main sheet winch," Sir Chay told me. "That was the answer."

If you took the largest main sheet winch that you could buy off the shelf, its size would dictate the breaking strength of the main sheet, which would then dictate the sail area of the mainsail, which would, in turn, dictate the overall size of the rig. And the size of the rig would dictate the volume of the hull and, therefore, the number of people you could fit in the hull. And so you had a vessel that ultimately was designed around the largest production winch available. This kept costs down, since none of the parts would require any custom labor; the whole boat could be built with production hardware.

This story is useful for the purposes of this book in deciding how you, the reader, would like to approach your sailing life. Sam Manning and I chose a boat design that best represents our approach to sailing, but everyone must decide for himself what best fits his approach. L. Francis Herreshoff declared in the opening pages of *The Compleat Cruiser* that he offers two such vessels in the book that represented two different approaches to "cruising"—one, a shallow-draft catboat named *Piscator*, which was a twenty-four-foot, converted small fishing catboat with a beam half as wide as its overall length, and *Viator*, a thirty-two-foot ketch. Both vessels are equipped with small wood/coal stoves, and their owners delight in exploring the Massachusetts coast in three seasons.

Of *Piscator*, one of Herreshoff's characters exclaimed: "By golly, sir, she is roomy and shallow, comfortable and handy and you can't beat that combination."

The joy these sailors experienced is the spirit of the book in your hands—the thrill of exploration and discovery, the satisfaction in honing one's seamanship skills, and the stirring warmth of sharing an adventure with a close friend or family member. The book is brimming with gems of seamanship skills, often presented as a narrative adventure.

Herreshoff suggests ways to rig an anchor so the flukes don't foul amid a chapter on how to make an authentic New England fish chowder.

Another book worth mentioning here is *Swallows and Amazons* by Arthur Ransome, the first in a series of adventure books for children that was published in the 1930s and '40s that inspired countless readers on small-boat voyages, real and imagined, for decades. The book opens with four children getting permission from their parents to sail to an island offshore by themselves aboard their little catboat, *Swallow*. They spend the ensuing weeks becoming consummate sailors and having a high time. Accordingly, we'll refer to the fictional boat in this book as *Swallow*, as a tribute to the simmering, exploring child spirit in all of us.

Where you sail can have a large impact on the design, of course. The shallow flats inside the Gulf waters of the Florida Keys or the sandy shallows of the Chesapeake might well suggest a centerboard sloop with a draft of a foot or less, especially if you can drag it up on a sandy beach for a picnic lunch. For me, sailing in Maine waters, it's a toss-up between the benefits of a full-keel boat versus one with a centerboard. With a full keel you can nose out of the bay in a heavy swell and around the bold cliffs of Monhegan on a breezy afternoon just as comfortably as you can explore the sheltered waters of Penobscot or Frenchman Bays. But with a shoal draft you can poke into the salt marshes and tidal flats and, my favorite, nose right up onto a sandy beach and hop ashore.

Some might wonder why I haven't suggested an outboard motor for a small sailboat. Plenty of people have them, slung like backpacks on the transom from handy brackets that pivot into place when the motor is needed. The answer is simple: because I hate them. They are temperamental, have tiny moving parts that make them difficult to service, and, unless you are the most assiduous maintenance person, they will fail when you need them most. I, for one, am too casual a person to take care of one of these motors well enough to trust one. Every time I have, nearly without exception, I have been disappointed. (An old friend of mine, who used to own a boatyard in Maine, once quipped, "There are three things in life I can do without: crying babies, barking dogs, and outboard motors.")

An inboard diesel, on the other hand, is strong and dependable. You can open the engine cover and access all sides. Change the oil, keep the battery charged, replace the sacrificial zincs regularly, and you have no trouble. It's really as simple as that. And winterizing takes less than an hour—running some nontoxic antifreeze through the intake lines, pulling out the impeller to relax its shape for the cold months, and pouring some anti-algae liquid into the fuel tanks and running it through the system.

Neither is the vessel portrayed in this book a "yacht." It's modeled after the small sailing workboats of the early 19th and 20th centuries, sturdy little craft that don't mind getting bumped or scraped. Varnish is for dandies. American marine historian Howard Chapelle offered a similar approach in his books and designs—small pleasure boats modeled on the workboat designs of coastal fishermen.

"The work-boats were developed by trial and error over a rather long period to meet the requirements of their use, within the limitations of low cost and the available materials," Chapelle wrote in his 1951 masterpiece *American Small Sailing Craft*. "It must be remembered that a work-boat is not left on her moorings when it blows, rains or snows, but must get out and help the owner earn his living."

The boat offered here is beautiful, but it is painted and oiled and can handle having lobster traps hauled into the cockpit as well as it can accommodate a passel of kids eating messy snacks and smearing their sunblock on the rails. A washdown with a bucket of seawater and a scrub brush will take care of it all.

—Twain Braden
Peaks Island, Maine, October 2012

LINE & KNOTS

"A thorough knowledge of marlinespike seamanship is of great importance to every seaman, as rope in its many forms is used constantly aboard ship . . . . He should also be able to tie the half dozen important knots in the dark."

—from *The American Merchant Seaman's Manual*

Camden Harbor is a glacial scoop out of the coast of Maine, a perfect, deepwater harbor sheltered on all sides, that served fleets of fishing vessels for hundreds of years—in the 20th century, all manner of yachts and working boats. A stream feeds into the harbor from the north in a picturesque waterfall that, in early spring, fishermen set up nets across to catch schools of smelts. Today, most of the workboats are gone, but Camden is a bustling little port, jammed with gleaming yachts along either edge of the harbor moored to hundreds of floats. You can sit at a seaside restaurant and watch the boat traffic—schooners refitted for the passenger trade, a few lobsterboats, and yachts of all sizes.

It was in that little harbor some years ago that I saw a middle-size yacht working its way into the narrow channel, the skipper, a red-faced man, gingerly feeling his way so as not to scrape his gelcoat against the protruding bowsprits and anchor flukes on one

Making a line off to a cleat ——

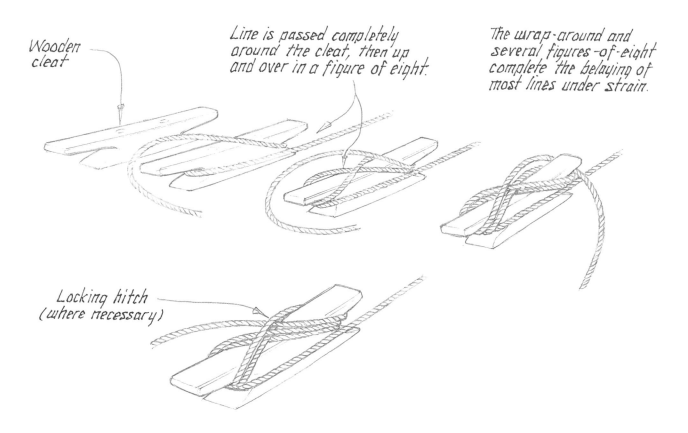

Wooden cleat

Line is passed completely around the cleat, then up and over in a figure of eight.

The wrap-around and several figures-of-eight complete the belaying of most lines under strain.

Locking hitch (where necessary)

side of him and the moored boats on the other. It was a tight fit and required all his attention. Meanwhile, a woman, presumably his wife, was stationed on deck about half-way forward, anxiously peering over the side and pointing nervously with one hand at looming boats that seemed a little close. In the other hand she held a tightly wrapped coil of line. From the jerky motions of the helm, it was clear the man was nervous and that his entrance into the harbor was probably his first. He'd turn a little one way, and then, fearing he'd turned too far, spin the wheel back hard in the other direction. Back and forth, his wife chattering and pointing the whole time as the boat glided toward the town dock.

It was clear from where I stood, on the deck of a schooner moored adjacent to the town float, that this couple was headed for trouble. It was also clear to about 100 other people in the harbor, sitting on benches along the waterfront or at the many open-air cafés. They stopped their reading or held their sandwiches midway to their mouths, all eyes fixed on this approaching yacht. When the boat was about fifty feet away, the woman seemed to remember the coil of line in her hand and started desperately clawing at the coil, just as the man gunned the engine astern. The boat lurched to a sudden stop—the woman on deck staggered—and came to rest nowhere near the dock. He then gunned it forward, and the boat crabbed another fifteen feet forward, twisting at an awkward angle to the dock. The woman, whose balance had been tested by the boat's motion, hadn't made much progress on the coil, and by this time the man was shouting.

"Throw the rope!"

A few more throttle and helm maneuvers later and the boat ended up perpendicular to the dock in a way that was anything but graceful. Meanwhile, a number of us dock-rats and other good Samaritans scrambled onto the dock and grabbed hold of the bow, managing to keep it from spearing the dock. We dragged it bodily alongside and held it steady while all the lines were uncoiled and—eventually—secured to the boat's cleats and dock's bollards. The man, livid and in a tight-lipped fury, was still sputtering at his wife (*Just give them the rope!*); the woman had assumed a kind of helpless, victim-like attitude, embarrassed at the spectacle and, no doubt, her husband's childlike behavior.

The hero to this little story should have been the coil of rope in the woman's hands. Had it, and a few others like it, been set up on deck a few minutes before their approach, the docking maneuver could have been relatively straightforward, if a little clumsy. The point is simply that a line coiled up in a tight gasket isn't much use in a hurry, whereas a line that is strategically placed can be salvation itself.

With few exceptions, rope aboard a vessel is called line. Consider rope as raw material: it comes in large spools from a factory, is still considered rope when it is in the chandlery, and becomes line only when you have selected it for a desired purpose and cut it to fit. Once it's slung over your shoulder and you're walking out of the chandlery, the rope that was once on the spool is suddenly a line—whether the main sheet, a dock line, or a halyard.

The learning of knots (and bends and hitches) is an activity to be taken seriously, but do not let yourself become frustrated. Basic knots that are useful aboard boats are simple and easy to learn. The novice sailor will often be intimidated by learning simple knots and, as a result, create a large tangle in a line in place of a simple knot, unwittingly adhering to the principle, "If you don't know a knot, tie a lot." But a tangle has the potential to damage the boat and endanger the crew—far simpler, then, to learn the few turns and tucks that a handful of simple knots require. This chapter will teach you how to tie these few knots, and knowing them will allow you to manage most basic tasks of seamanship that running a small sailboat will require. In general, unless attempting decoration, use the simplest knot; it is probably the best for the task.

If you're interested in learning more about knots, including how to tie decorative and fancy knots, there are numerous volumes available. The most comprehensive is *The Ashley Book of Knots*, published in 1944 and still in print around the world. It is a celebration—a massive, fully illustrated tome—of every conceivable knot in existence. But it can be a little overwhelming to the novice. A more practical introductory book is Hervey Garrett Smith's *The Arts of the Sailor*. This is perhaps the one necessary knot-and-splice book, since its selection of knots and drawings separate the unnecessary chaff from the valuable wheat. The drawings are simple and offered in clear sequence so even the clumsiest person can follow along to tie knots and splice rope.

This chapter, as with every other subject, takes the minimalist approach, suggesting a few simple knots, hitches, bends, splices, and some notes on handling line so that you can get started on a boat right away. But take the time to learn these simple tasks, and your sailing life will be the richer for it.

THREE-STRAND AND BRAIDED ROPE

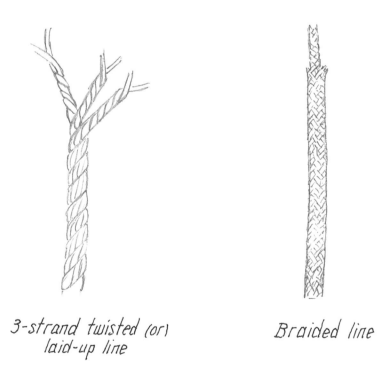

3-strand twisted (or) laid-up line

Braided line

Twisted, or laid, rope has been made for thousands of years. Twisted rope is typically comprised of three strands that are twisted tightly, usually clockwise, so that the twist holds the rope together. Traditionally made of manila, hemp, or cotton, the raw material of twisted rope today is mostly man made. Yet for some 10,000 years it was made of the natural, stringy fibers of plants, laid out in, typically, three, great, twisted strands and then twisted together. Some credit the Ancient Egyptians for the first twisted rope, which was made of twisted river reeds; others, the Chinese. There is still a narrow alley south of Broad St. in Charleston, S.C., that carries the name of its original purpose: Ropemaker's Lane.

Braided rope, which has a core and an outer, braided-fiber skin, is common for recreational use. It is easier on the hands than twisted (or "laid") rope because of its soft—and more even—outer layer. For better or worse, twisted rope tends to stretch more than braided rope. Both braided and twisted rope are made of many different materials, including Dacron, nylon, and polypropylene. There are also many high-tech fibers that are available for the performance-oriented sailor, such as Kevlar, Spectra, Dyneema, and Vectran. These are extremely lightweight and do not stretch, making them more akin to steel wire, except that they are supple like other rope fibers. The following is a description of basic rope types today. The man made ropes listed are designed both to be strong and to resist rot from moisture and ultraviolet decay.

1. Polypropylene

    Polypropylene, also called polypro or poly, is an all-purpose, inexpensive rope that has a distinctive, plastic-like feel. It stretches, making it unsuitable for use as running rigging. It can be used for docking lines or mooring pennants, since it will absorb great loads without coming up taut suddenly; rather, it can stretch somewhat under a heavy load. But it's tendency to become stiff and bristly makes it an unpleasant rope to work with. Polypro does not hold knots well and becomes tangled easily.

    One benefit of polypro is that it floats. It makes an ideal towrope, or a passable dinghy painter, for this reason. Another smart use of polypro is as a "heaving line" (see sidebar), since it is so lightweight.

2. Nylon

    Nylon stretches and does not float. It is more expensive than polypro, but it holds up better against the sun and salt, and maintains a supple feel. Nylon has a slick, slippery look to it when new and is easy to splice, although its slipperiness does mean that a tight splice is something of a challenge. Nylon is an excellent choice for docking lines, as the stretching will help absorb shock. For this reason, nylon, especially twisted, is also a good choice for anchor rode or mooring pennants. Picture a vessel pitching at its mooring in a storm, constantly straining against the mooring pennant. You want a line that can absorb this kind of strain. Twisted nylon can stretch anywhere from 15 percent to 30 percent of its length (at roughly half of its breaking strength) and still remain undamaged. Braided nylon stretches less, less than 15 percent.

3. Dacron (Terylene)

Dacron does not stretch very much, making it an excellent candidate for running rigging, such as sheets and halyards. It stays supple to the touch and has good UV-resistance qualities. Dacron, whether twisted or braided, stretches about 10 percent of its length at half its working load. Dacron is also easy to splice. Because it is not slippery like nylon, Dacron splices will hold together well. If you can afford it, Dacron is probably the best choice for most of your boat's working lines, especially sheets and halyards.

4. Manila

While not as common as it was even twenty years ago, manila line can still be purchased at many chandleries. A natural fiber, manila is not as strong as modern synthetics, but its distinctive feel and exceptional handling characteristics make it a pleasure to work with and enhances the ambience of any classic boat. Manila is easy to splice, but it swells when wet, making knots difficult to remove and the line jam in sheaves. Manila should be inspected frequently for rot and wear.

5. Dyneema

Dyneema and other exceedingly lightweight rope material known under different brands, is worth pointing out here for its use as running rigging. These high-tech fibers usually make up the core of the rope, where their strength is needed most. The more basic lines above are inexpensive and capable of serving in all the capacities needed on a boat. However, the more modern lines are considerably lighter, don't absorb water, and degrade less in UV light. It's hard to argue with that kind of performance. The only reason to consider alternatives is price, since cost of these lines is ghastly for the cost-conscious sailor. Yet if you're going to consider a lightweight line, it's best to put it to its most effective use and that would be as jib sheets, where the lightweight will not tug downward on the foil shape of the sail, especially in light air.

DOCK LINES

Any boat (excepting small dinghies and others such as Lasers, 420s, and Sunfish) should have at least four lines dedicated to securing the vessel to a dock. Nylon is an excellent choice for making dock lines, as the inherent stretch in the line, especially if it is twisted rope, will make any docking maneuver less jerky. (Note that Dacron line will not stretch and therefore is not a great choice for dock lines.)

Each dock line should have an eye splice in one end and a whipping on the other. When approaching a dock, always cast the eye of the line to the person on the dock, and direct him or her to pass the eye around the dock's cleat or post. Placing the splice around the post enables the crew of the boat to apply tension or ease the line in a manner that is consistent with what the helmsman or skipper requires. Always set up your dock line well in advance of the actual maneuvers, picturing how the lines will ultimately be configured when the boat is resting alongside the dock. Consider using chafe gear at the hawseholes—the holes in the bulkwarks of the boat where the anchor chain or dock lines pass through—or chocks if a harbor is especially rough and wave-action extreme.

CHAFE

If allowed to rest and rub against another object, line will begin to chafe. If allowed to chafe long enough, the individual fibers become lacerated, and the rope will eventually cut through. Guarding against chafe is a constant worry aboard a boat. You should prevent or guard against chafe whenever possible.

Dock and mooring lines are especially prone to chafe. When a vessel is alongside, it will roll and pitch, causing the lines to be repeatedly drawn up tight and then slack, and then tight again. This back-and-forth motion causes the line to chafe against the hawseholes. Even a relatively secure dock can cause chafe in dock lines if the lines are not rotated, periodically adjusted, or protected.

How to guard against chafe? There are several methods, depending on the function of the line. Most involve introducing a sacrificial layer of fabric. Canvas or surplus firehose—which is canvas on the outside and rubber on the inside—can be wrapped around the line in the area where it will chafe against the boat, thereby protecting the rope itself. Firehose is an excellent option; the rubberized interior grips well against the rope, but the fabric exterior slides on the hawse. Expired hose can often be procured from fire stations; a hose that may be retired from fighting fires for safety reasons still makes excellent chafe protection. Chafe can also take place in a boat's rig. Sails can chafe against running backstays or other rigging. Sheets can chafe against lifelines or stays. Even sheaves chafe the lines they serve just by being in constant contact at the same part of the line. It is often advisable to "end-for-end" a boat's running rigging—this means reversing the line so that different sections of the same line come to bear on the sheaves and cleats. Halyards and sheets are both good candidates for an end-for-end treatment. Just be sure to use a secure tagline when doing this with a halyard; otherwise it will be necessary to send a person aloft to reroute a line. Be on guard against chafe constantly— while sailing, at anchor, and even alongside the dock.

A ROUND TURN

A round turn is an extra turn in a line taken around a ring or grommet that distributes the load on the line where it is in contact with the ring. A round turn is used as chafe protection.

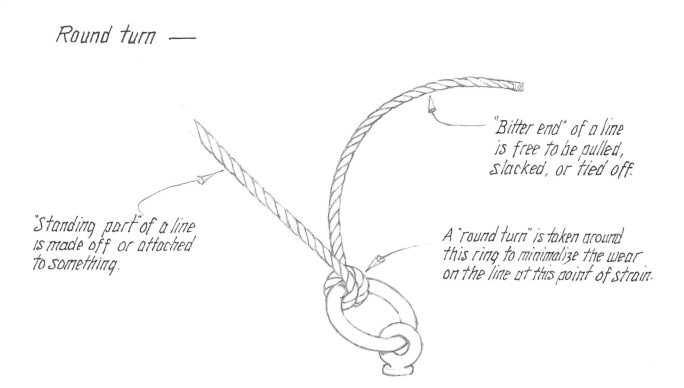

Round turn —

"Bitter end" of a line is free to be pulled, slacked, or tied off.

"Standing part" of a line is made off or attached to something.

A "round turn" is taken around this ring to minimalize the wear on the line at this point of strain.

BAGGYWRINKLE

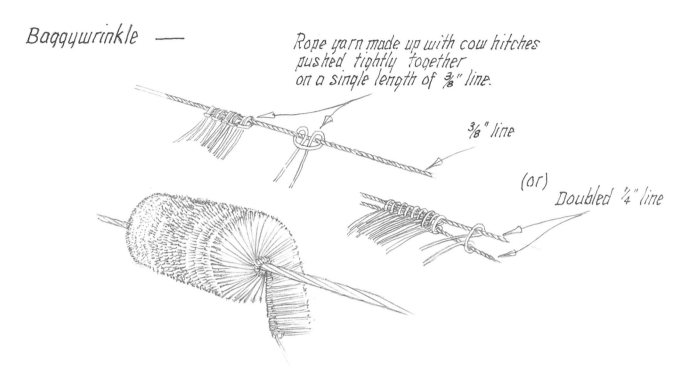

Baggywrinkle —

Rope yarn made up with cow hitches pushed tightly together on a single length of ⅜" line.

⅜" line

(or) Doubled ¼" line

Although it sounds like a disparaging term for a person who is getting on in years, baggywrinkle actually refers to traditional chafe gear that is installed in a boat's rig. When sails come to bear against running backstays or shrouds, they chafe, potentially wearing holes or creating weak spots in the fabric. Clumps of fuzzy baggywrinkle secured to a boat's standing rigging eliminate—or at least significantly reduce—the amount of chafe that occurs as a result of this action.

To make a baggywrinkle, secure both ends of an eight-foot length of three-eighths-of-an-inch line to a stationary object. (If you're doing this on your boat, secure the line to the lifelines or between the shrouds.) Cut up a three-strand rope in numerous, eight-inch sections. Unlay the rope sections so that you are left with a large pile of the individual strands. Now, using a cow hitch, secure these strands, one at a time, to the longer line that you have secured between your shrouds, beginning at one end and working down the line. Each successive cow hitch should be tied snugly against the one previously laid on.

Once you've created a six- to eight-foot section of this hairy mass, it is time to install it in the rig. Using a bosun's chair, hoist yourself into the rig and seize one end of this line to the shroud in the area where chafe is likely to occur. Now wrap the baggywrinkle around the shroud tightly, completely covering the shroud so that the strands all stick straight out from the shroud. Once you've finished, seize the bottom of the baggywrinkle securely to the shroud as you did the upper end.

TO LOCK OR NOT TO LOCK

Each time you make a line off to a cleat or pin, you will wrap several figures of eight. On a belay pin, three turns is considered standard; any more and you'll be making a mess.

Should you use a locking hitch? A locking hitch is made by flipping the bight (loop) of a line over on itself when making it off to a cleat or a pin. It is a very secure arrangement, and, if made tight enough, it will not slip. But is one needed every time? This depends on the boat and how secure a line is without a locking hitch, but the standard on working sailing ships involves using a locking hitch on a halyard when there's a man aloft whose life depends on the line being secure.

Many vessel skippers choose not to use locking hitches on sheets and halyards, the theory being that, if the line is to be taken off in a hurry (as in a knockdown or approaching squall), a locking hitch will unnecessarily slow the process. But using a locking hitch on a gantline—a line used for raising a person aloft—will give pause to anyone who might be working on deck, tidying lines. If he sees a locking hitch on a line where there is strain, he'll be less likely to simply cast it off. (At least, that's the idea.)

A locking hitch may also be appropriate for use on docking lines or on lines which are secured to a cleat that might be too small to make enough wraps to be fully secure.

THE BITTER END

This may sound like the name of a rough-and-tumble bar for sailors. Actually, the "bitter end" refers to the end of a length of line. Most lines, whether sheets or halyards, have a standing end—the end that is attached to the sail or another object—and a bitter end—an end that is not attached to anything. This is useful to know when instructing someone handling line on deck, making a sheet off on a pin or cleat or coiling down a halyard, for example. If someone can understand the difference between the bitter end and standing end (the end of the line attached to something) it makes more complex instructions, maneuvers, or sail trimming, much easier.

Line made off to a belaying pin ——

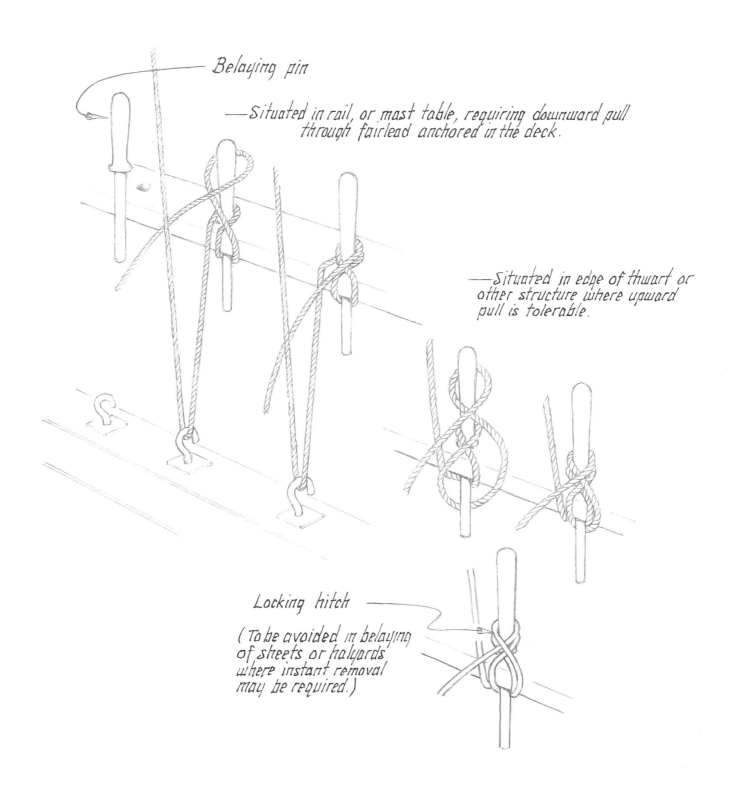

Belaying pin

—Situated in rail, or mast table, requiring downward pull
through fairlead anchored in the deck.

—Situated in edge of thwart or
other structure where upward
pull is tolerable.

Locking hitch ——

(To be avoided in belaying
of sheets or halyards
where instant removal
may be required.)

Heaving Lines and Monkey's Fists

A heaving line is a lightweight line that is weighted on one end with a monkey's fist and, on the other end, secured to a dock line with a simple bend. Heaving lines are handy to use when you are approaching a dock in windy conditions or tight quarters. By securing a heaving line to your dock line—which is heavier and much more difficult to throw any great distance—you can incorporate the assistance of people on the dock to assist in your docking maneuvers.

To set up a heaving line, first tie off your monkey's fist to one end of a fifty-foot length of line. Polypro is a sensible choice for use as a heaving line because it floats. Anyone who has docked a boat in difficult circumstances can appreciate the number of times that the dock line lands just short of the dock and promptly sinks out of reach of the person on the dock. A heaving line should be lightweight, no more than about one-fourth to three-eighths of an inch in diameter. (Rope is measured in diameter, whereas wire is measured in circumference.)

Tie the other end of the heaving line to the eye splice of your dock line, using a slippery rolling hitch. Before the actual approach, the person handling the line should set up the docking line so that it will not foul as it runs out to the dock. Once the heaving line and dock lines are set up, make a neat coil in the heaving line, and then split the coil so that half of it is in one hand and the other half—the one with the monkey's fist—is in your throwing hand.

The command from the skipper or helmsman should be something along the lines of, "Toss it when you can"—that is, when you think you are close enough to the dock to actually reach it with an easy toss. When you toss, imagine that you are throwing a discus. This is a sidearm throw, one that requires plenty of room to swing. Throw the line in a high arc in the general vicinity of the person on the dock. Don't try to hit him with the line; try to throw the line past him so that he can catch the line as the monkey's fist sails past. (You don't want to nail him with the monkey's fist; then he's no good to you whatsoever, lying unconscious on the dock.)

Instruct the dockhand to do no more than place the eye splice of the dock line around the dock's cleat or bitt. Many dockhands, in attempts to be helpful, will attempt to haul your boat when they've captured a line. It is far easier for the boat crew to manage the difficult procedure of bringing the boat alongside with the use of lines. Besides, they are more likely to hear the commands (and be interested in their subject) of the helmsman than a person on the dock.

Some useful tools

- A marlinespike is a tapered piece of steel, which can be used to open the cant of the line for a splice, to loosen or tighten a knot, or as a lever for loosening shackles. Most marlinespikes have a flattened tip like a slotted screwdriver, making them easy to slip between knots and strands of rope.
- A fid is a wooden marlinespike. A Swedish fid is a hollowed-out fid with a metal shaft, which makes splicing easier since you can slip the grooved, steel shaft between the strands. It can be used to open a gap between two strands of rope, leaving the hollow channel to insert another strand. Swedish fids typically have wooden handles for comfort.
- A knife is an essential tool for seamanship and line handling. A knife with a fixed or locking blade will work best, as it will not collapse on your fingers. Keep the edge sharp, as a dull blade is more dangerous—and far less useful—than one with a keen blade. A serrated edge will cut through line quickly, but the edge is difficult—nigh impossible—to sharpen without specialized equipment.
- A pair of slim pliers with gripping teeth is often helpful when working with knots and splices.
- A leather palm, which fits over the user's dominant hand, is like a giant thimble. It is used to press large sailmaker's needles through heavy sailcloth or rope. The palm's metal cup is grooved to hold the head of a needle.
- A sailmaker's needle is a heavy, steel sewing needle for repairing sails and whipping the ends of line or making seizings. The needle's tip is usually shaped in an elongated triangle. A sailmaker's needle has a large eye for heavy thread.
- A chunk of natural beeswax can be used to protect twine or thread when repairing sails or whipping lines. Run the thread through the block of wax before

sewing. The wax will also hold stitches together, keeping the repairs tight, strong, and protected from the elements.

- A cigarette lighter is useful for burning the ends of certain plastic-based rope (such as nylon, polypropylene, and Dacron) so that the fibers melt together and therefore cannot unravel.

- Plastic electrical tape is useful for holding the ends of rope together when performing whippings or splices. Remove the tape when a splice or whip is completed.

MAKING A COIL

When you step aboard a boat, you'll know instantly whether the boat is well kept by one glance at the deck and cockpit. If lines are hanging neatly from their cleats and belay pins in uniformly-sized loops, you have a pretty good indication that the skipper cares about safety and order. If, on the contrary, you see a messy array of tangled line littering the deck like writhing snakes, turn around and walk back up the dock and find another sailing companion. It's that simple.

Coils should always be made clockwise. This tradition started when all rope was twisted with a right-hand lay. Coiling clockwise kept the line from untwisting and fouling. Today it still makes sense to coil line, twisted and braided, clockwise, since having a single coiling standard onboard will ensure uniformity.

To coil a halyard after a sail is set, grab the line at the standing end with one hand—your left if you are right-handed. Draw out a length of line with the right hand, giving it a half-turn in a clockwise direction with your fingers as you make a bight. Grab the new loop with your left hand and repeat the process. The half-turn works the kinks out of the line. The loops should all be the same size—large enough so you aren't left with an enormous pile of line and small enough that the loops don't spill all over the deck and pose a tripping hazard. Traditionally, all lines were coiled in such a way as to not touch the deck when they were hung on a belay pin.

To hang a coil on a pin or a cleat, reach one hand through the coil, grabbing a bight from the standing end and pulling it through the coil. Turn the bight over once in your hand before capturing the coil, and then hang the bight back on a horn of the cleat or belay pin.

To coil 3-strand twisted rope ——

The line being coiled is given a clockwise twist with each loop
to prevent kinks from forming.

For stowage, the coil is given
wraps around the middle
with the loose or "bitter"
end.

To end the wrapping, a bight of the bitter end
is pulled through, looped over the top and
pulled down tight.

To put a gasket on a coiled line for stowing ——

3-strand laid line.
Right-hand lay.

Laid line of a right-hand lay
is coiled in a clockwise direction.

Right-hand-lay line
coils without kinks
if the rope itself is
given a clockwise twist
for each turn of the coil.

Ties or gaskets are
cinched around the
coiled line to hold its
shape during stowage
below decks.

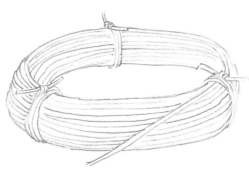

The coil is cinched together amidships
with its own bitter end.

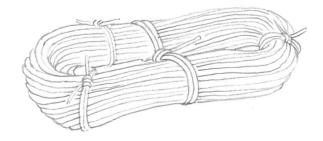

A good habit to establish is coiling down all your halyards immediately after all the sails are set. This way they are off the deck during the course of the day when you need to handle sheets while tacking or gybing. You don't want your sheets commingling with your halyards.

A KNOT, A HITCH, OR A BEND?

Most people don't pause to consider the differences between a knot, a hitch, or a bend. While similar in appearance, each differs in function. A knot is formed when a single line turns back onto itself, such as to form a loop (bowline); a bend is when two different lines are joined together (fisherman's bend); and a hitch is when a line attaches to something else, such as a spar or mooring bitt (clove hitch). As explained in the ensuing examples, each has its own specific use.

COMMON KNOTS

1. Bowline: This is the most common sailor's knot. Relatively easy to tie—with some practice—the bowline is also easy to untie, even if a heavy load has been imposed on the line. A bowline can be used to secure a sheet to the grommet on the clew of a sail, to secure a downhaul or a halyard, or to make a secure loop in a dinghy's painter—indeed, the bowline can be used for just about any purpose where a secure loop is required.

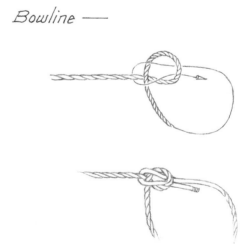

Bowline ——

   If tying off a bowline for a purpose that might allow for chafe—as on a sheet or a halyard, for example—use a round turn on the bight of the line before securing the bitter end of the knot. This will spread out the load of the line and hence reduce any resulting chafe, keeping your line in good condition.

   Tie a bowline repeatedly until your hands know the knot. First, tie the bowline until you can do it with your eyes shut, then tie it behind your back, then learn to tie it with one hand. Once you do this, your hands will never forget the motion, and they'll be able to tie a bowline in a hurry when they need to.

2. Reef knot: A reef knot is used to secure the bottom of a sail when it is time to reef. A reef knot—called a "square knot" ashore—is two overhand knots, but the second overhand knot is tied opposite the first. If tied improperly, a "granny knot" is the result; granny knots are two overhand knots, but they look lopsided.

A reef knot, unlike a granny knot, will always untie easily when the knot is pushed together on itself. A slippery reef knot is when one loop is left in the knot, allowing the knot to remain secure but also to be pulled out easily.

When securing reef points, be sure to secure them between the boltrope of the sail and the boom, not going around the base of the boom even if the reef points are long enough. The sailmaker has built "roach" into the sail's panels. If you lash the foot of the

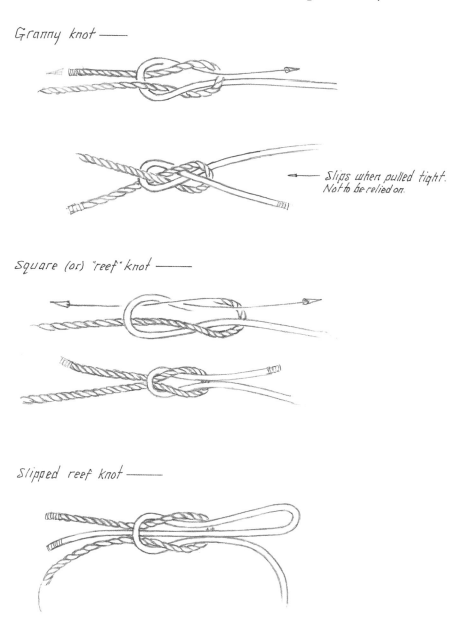

Granny knot

Slips when pulled tight.
Not to be relied on.

Square (or) "reef" knot

Slipped reef knot

sail to the boom with the reef knots, the roach is eliminated and the sail becomes too flat, less like the foil shape it needs to provide lift.

3. Constrictor knot: Although it is really a hitch, as it is used to secure a line to an object other than a rope—such as a post or the neck of a sailbag—the constrictor knot is handy because, not only will it not slip, it will become tighter as a strain is applied but not loosen when the strain is relieved. It can be used to temporarily secure a cracked tiller or oar, or simply to tie a small line around a pencil so that it won't leave the nav station.

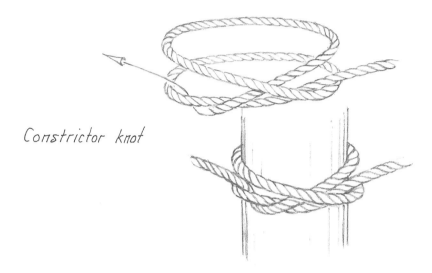

Constrictor knot

4. Figure-of-eight knot: A figure-of-eight knot is tied to the bitter end of a line that you do not want to allow to slip through the block. The figure-of-eight, when drawn up tight, forms a tidy ball at the end of the line, preventing the line from running all the way out. This is a helpful knot to tie on the end of a main or jib sheet, for example.

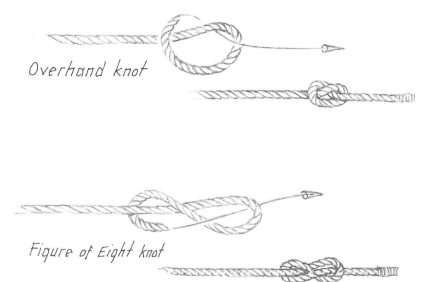

Overhand knot

Figure of Eight knot

5. Stopper knot: This might technically qualify as a bend or even a hitch, since its purpose is to take the strain off another line, but that's the beauty of the English language—its exceptions and variety. The stopper is great for taking the strain off a sheet or halyard jammed in a winch or block. Knowing how to make a stopper knot when you need one will make you the hero of the moment.

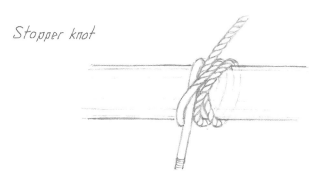

Stopper knot

The stopper was traditionally used on the decks of sailing ships with a dedicated line secured to the deck. The line, about three or four feet long, had one end spliced into an eyebolt on deck near the belay pin that serviced a halyard. The line was then untwisted and rebraided—like a ponytail in long hair—back together so that the shape and feel of the line was flatter and softer. (The bitter end was whipped.) When a sail was raised by large teams of sailors in the days before winches, this line was employed by securing a simple "friction hitch" around the straining halyard, above where the belay pin was, held in place with one hand, while the other hand was used to make the halyard off to the belay pin.

COMMON BENDS

1. Sheet bend: The sheet bend is the most widely practiced means of joining two lines together. Its simplicity and functionality are perfect. Begin the knot by passing the working end of one of the lines through the bight of another line. Wrap it around the back side of the bight, coming back around to the front. Instead of passing the line through the bight again, wrap it under itself, and bring it up to pull tight.

Sheet bend

2. Fisherman's bend: A fisherman's bend is the simplest bend to make when joining two lines of equal diameter, especially when you want to be able to adjust the tension without undoing the line. A fisherman's bend can be doubled or tripled for added security and snugness.

Fisherman's bend

3. Anchor bend: More of a hitch than a bend, the anchor bend was traditionally used to secure a line to the ring of an anchor. It is fast and easy to set up and will not come undone.

Anchor bend

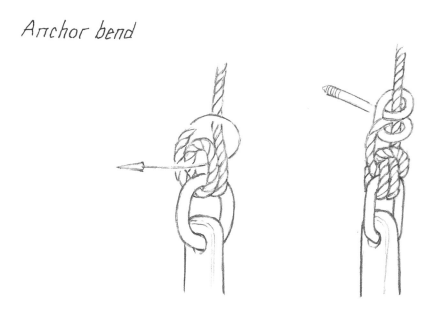

COMMON HITCHES

1. Half hitch: A half hitch is ubiquitous for its simplicity. It involves making a single turn around the standing end of a line, and passing the line back through the bight.

Two half hitches are an excellent choice for securing a fender to a stanchion on approach to a dock. They can be tied and untied easily.

Half hitch

2 Half hitches

2. Clove hitch: A clove hitch is handy to use as an all-purpose hitch for securing a dinghy to a post or piling. The clove hitch will not hold if there is a variable strain—a good alternative would be a pair of half hitches. What's nice about a clove hitch, though, is that it is an easy and attractive way to secure a line to a post in a way that effectively doubles the surface area of the bight of line in a more secure way than a simple loop would. But because a clove hitch can slip under strain, you can use a clove hitch backed by two half hitches to get the benefits of each knot together.

Clove hitch

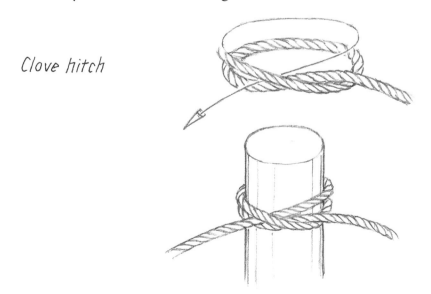

3. Rolling hitch: A rolling hitch is a variant of the stopper knot, excellent for securing a line to a post or spar that will not slide or release under strain. Be sure that you tie the hitch in such a way that the strain is applied in the same direction as the hitch's two initial wraps. This makes use of the added friction of the doubled wraps.

Rolling hitch

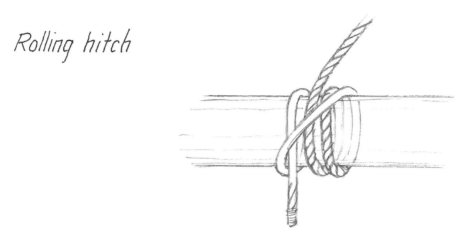

4. Cow hitch: To make a cow hitch, pass a bight of line around whatever it is you want to secure it to, then pass the bitter ends through the loop. (You can also do this with a spliced loop.) A cow hitch is ideal for securing a "tell tale" to a sail or the numerous short strands of line that make up the hairy mass of baggywrinkle.

Cow hitch

5. Trucker's hitch: A trucker's hitch, as the name implies, is especially handy for securing cargo, since it allows you to apply a great deal of strain on the line and then secure it—sort of like a block and tackle. The idea is to create a small loop in the standing end of the line, take a turn around an anchor point such as an eyebolt, and then pass

the bitter end through the loop. Haul on the bitter end as tight as you want, securing it with a couple of half hitches.

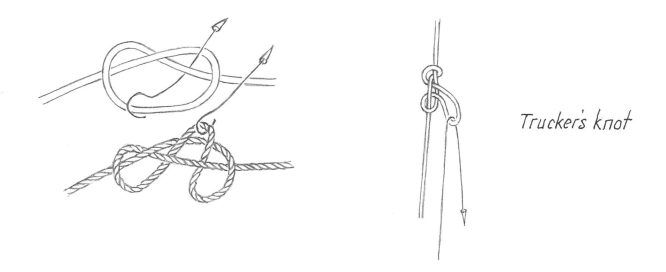

Trucker's knot

SEIZING

Siezing — with ends of small stuff pulled under.

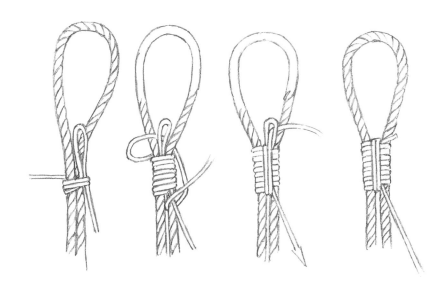

To seize a splice is to wrap it with "small stuff" or twine in such a way as to capture and squeeze the line together to form a tight bight or loop. By seizing the line, you effectively close the bight of the splice onto an object, such as a thimble or eyebolt, so the splice does not slip off.

ROPE CARE

Like every piece of equipment about a boat, rope needs to be cared for. This is somewhat less true than in times past, when natural fiber rope could not be stored wet or it would rot. (Although the rule is still true today even for artificial rope, though for different reasons: the line will mildew, even if it won't rot.) However, rope is still subject to the same laws of physics that affect the rest of the boat, so even the most modern materials wear out and need to be checked regularly for chafe and stretch damage. Line that becomes stiff from repeated strain or UV damage becomes difficult to coil and handle, and nearly impossible to splice.

Inspection of your boat's lines is a necessity. Periodically run each line through your fingers, visually inspecting the entire length, looking for chafed areas or cut fibers. If the rope is twisted rope, twist open the strands and inspect the inside of the rope where the strands wear against each other. If the individual strand's edges have become pointed and are worn to the degree that small bits of fiber are coming away from the strands, the rope is at the end of its useful life and must be retired.

There is no rule of thumb dictating how often a line needs to be replaced, as this is dependant on the environment, the amount of sailing done, how it is stored, and its specific use. But a line should remain supple to the touch and able to be turned comfortably around a pin or cleat without feeling stiff.

WHIPPING

Whipping is done to the bitter end of a rope so that the strands do not unravel. This is another clue about how well kept a boat is. If the bitter ends of lines are frayed and perhaps held together with some worn electrical or duct tape, the rigger or owner hasn't taken the time to finish the job. Every single line in use on a boat—from the bell rope to the halyards and sheets to the docking lines to the anchor rode—should have a whipping on the bitter end.

There are two basic methods of making a whip on the end of a line. One involves using a needle to make a secure, long-lasting whip; the other is called a "quick-whip" and can be made without a needle. Both styles of whipping should be made extremely tight so that they cannot become unraveled. An added measure of protection, at least on nylon, polypro, and Dacron, is to melt the bitter end with a cigarette lighter so that the strands solidify into a single plug.

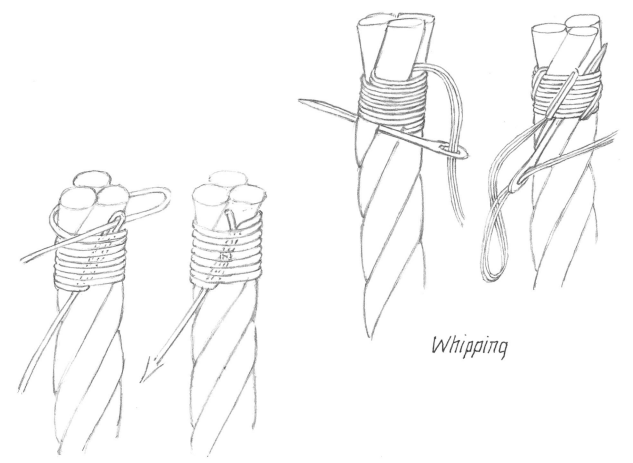

Whipping

Temporary whipping made like a siezing with ends of the small stuff pulled under.

To make a quick whip, make a simple bight in the thread, laying it against and parallel to the line near the bitter end. Now, begin to wrap the thread around the line, working from the standing end toward the bitter end so that the whipping of the thread covers the loop of the thread that has already been laid down. Make each wrap exceedingly tight, using a marlinespike to tighten the thread if necessary. Continue whipping the line until your whipping measures the same distance as the rope's diameter—for example, make the whip a half-inch long if the rope is half-inch diameter. When you've whipped far enough, pass the end of the thread through the loop, then draw the loop up tight so that the loop is drawn under the whipping. Cut the thread at both ends so that the loop is buried beneath the whipping.

To make a more permanent whipping, begin the whip in the same manner, but remember that a loop is unnecessary. Whip the line to the same distance as the rope's diameter, then use the needle to bring the line back across the whipping, following the cant (groove) of the line. Perform two of these "frappings" for each of the rope's three cants; then bury the end of the thread and cut it off closely.

SPLICING THREE-STRAND ROPE

Eye-splice in 3-strand laid-up line

Splicing is another of those skills that you should practice until your hands learn the motions. And it's another of those skills that tends to separate amateurs from the experts.

If a line is going to be permanently used with a bight of line in the same place, it makes sense to splice the loop. All knots weaken the rope's overall strength. A splice done properly recovers some of that strength. Plus, a splice is smooth and attractive. If a splice is being used in the rigging and a small, concentrated strain is going to be imposed on the loop, consider using a thimble in the splice. A thimble is a rounded metal or nylon ring that is formed to fit the inside of a splice. Be sure that the thimble you select is of the same diameter as the line with which it will be used. Otherwise, the thimble will fall out—probably at the worst possible moment.

Splicing is confusing the first few times it is attempted. There are a few rules of thumb to learn:

- Three-strand rope is spliced by sending the strands against the lay of the line. You want to splice such that all three strands are advanced together—that is, tuck one strand once, then tuck the others in turn.
- A basic splice involves tucking each of the strands three times. The outcome of this should be that all three strands emerge from the standing end of the line at the same place in the line.
- To finish the splice, advance one of the tucks one more time beyond where the basic splice was finished, then advance a second strand two more times beyond the end of the splice. This produces a splice with a tapered look. Another method is to continue to tuck all the strands in the same method as the initial splice, but not before cutting a percentage of the strand (about one-third) with a knife. By the time three more tucks are made with each strand, the splice will have a long, even taper both attractive and functional in its design.

MAKING A PENNANT FOR A WASH-DOWN BUCKET

Every boat should have a wash-down bucket—one that you can toss over the side and retrieve with a length of line so you can rinse the deck. The best bucket for a small boat is a collapsible canvas variety, which stores easily. Or you can use a plastic or rubber masonry bucket with a swinging metal handle. Do not use a metal bucket, however, as it will rust and scratch the side of the hull.

To make a pennant for a bucket using three-strand rope, first tie a clove hitch to the handle on one end of an eight-foot length of line (at least a half-inch in diameter) of any material. The two loops of the clove hitch will spread out the purchase of the line on the handle and reduce chafe. Now unwrap the working end of the line close to the clove hitch, and splice it back into the standing end. Tying single overhand knots into the line at regular intervals—say, every two feet—will ease the raising of the bucket onto the deck of the boat. Finish the end with an eye splice or decorative knot.

Be sure to have a firm grip on the bucket's leash (but don't tie it to your wrist) when throwing it over the side of a moving boat. The bucket will act as a sea anchor and can pull you over the side or at least pull it from your grasp. Always use extreme caution when bringing a bucket aboard so as not to lose balance.

ABOARD *SWALLOW*

Our fictional sloop, *Swallow*, will have all the lines above—halyards that raise and lower the sails, sheets that trim them, and a set of docking lines. Each boat needs at least four docking lines. They should be designated for this purpose and this purpose only, stored in a locker in the cockpit and available for quick use. Having a stash of spare line of various lengths is also a good idea. You never know when you'll need to extend the length of your anchor rode, tie your boat to a tree to ride out a storm, or help a neighbor in distress with a tow.

2

SAILBOAT ANATOMY

"Voyaging on board a small, well-found vessel is a unique way to slide gently into other people's lives, then move onward again with time to savour what you have seen and learned. Because, in a world more rushed than ever by the ticking of a clock, life afloat moves at a pace that is humane and natural."

—from *Saraffyn's Mediterranean Adventure,* by Lin and Larry Pardey

sabel Kwel was a large ocean-going tugboat that operated in the North Atlantic and North Sea in the 1930s and '40s, ultimately serving the Allied forces on the Murmansk Run—the voyage for madmen that enabled Nazi pilots and U-boat crews to slaughter Allied supply ships and their escorts as neatly as shooting fish in a barrel. She was a fictional vessel, the platform for Jan de Hartog's classic book, *The Captain,* but she was based on numerous such tugs that served the Murmansk Run between Great Britain and the Russian ports of Murmansk and Archangel, across the Barents and White Seas.

Isabel Kwel carried an enormous diesel, a single screw beast that packed some 15,000 hp. She was capable of towing the largest commercial vessels afloat in the first half of the 20th century across oceans without refueling. The captain of the title was Martinus

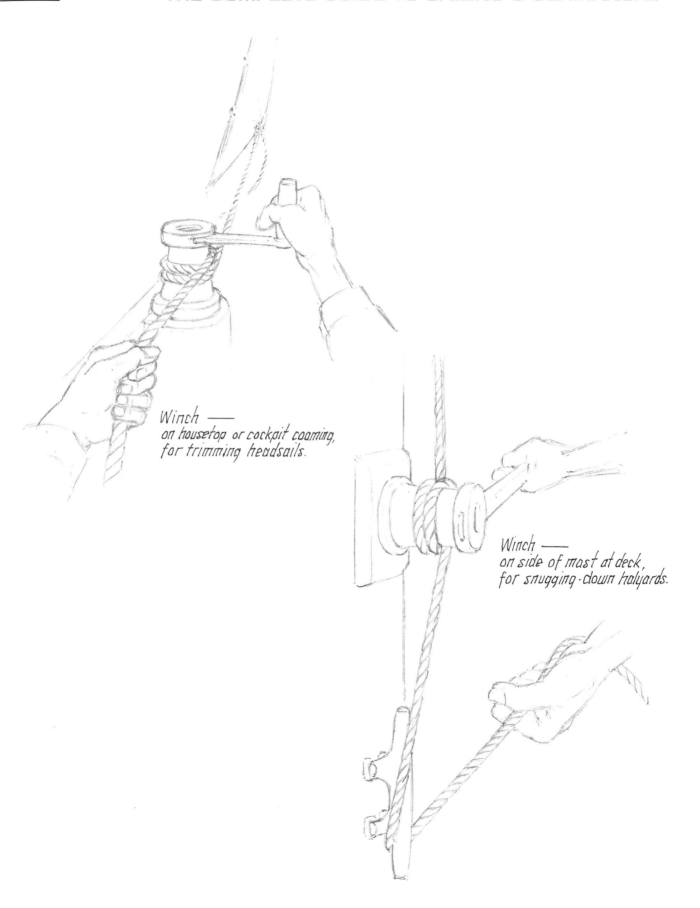

Winch ———
on housetop or cockpit coaming,
for trimming headsails.

Winch ———
on side of mast at deck,
for snugging-down halyards.

Harinxma, a cocky young Dutchman thrust unwillingly into the leadership role during a time when the British desperately needed seamen to run convoy ships through the Axis defenses to resupply hungry troops and starving populations of eastern cities under siege. The British dragooned Dutchmen, renowned for their seagoing prowess and now without a country because of the German occupation, by the thousands.

Harinxma was not even thirty years old when he was given command of *Isabel Kwel* by the conniving and rat-faced Mr. Kwel, who knew Harinxma had the intelligence and natural ability to handle the vessel. But Harinxma quickly learned he had to work much harder to earn the respect of her professional crew. His biggest fear was being laughed off the tug, ignored for his youth, and made a mockery. In response he soon developed an aloof alter ego that insulated him from the crew and eventually earned him their respect.

One trick of his was to utter vague non sequiturs when presented with puzzling situations. "Fancy that," he would say when one of the crew tried to flummox him by staging an awkward prank. "Fancy that," he would say when blood ran the decks and bombs were dropping all around the vessel. *Fancy That* became his moniker among the crew, and they quickly developed awe for his enigmatic leadership—"superb sailor, uncanny knowledge of human nature, cool as they come, mordant wit, brilliant mind." In his own mind he remained well aware of his woeful inexperience, terrified that he'd be exposed as a fake, and, while comfortable with his skills handling ships, constantly aware of his need to maintain this alter ego to keep a fragile order on the ship.

What vexed him, though—and here is the point of this story—was a mysterious problem with the ship that he discovered during a simple docking maneuver in the first few days of his command. It was night, and he intended to pull the tug alongside another vessel, starboard side to, in the western Scottish port of Greenock. Moving at about half speed, he approached at a 45-degree angle, ordered the helm hard over to port at the crucial moment and, at the same time, the engine-order telegraph to half astern—a simple maneuver that would cause the stern to swing neatly alongside the moored vessel and, simultaneously, the headway of the heavy vessel to be checked by the enormous backward-swirling propeller. A deckhand would be able to step nimbly aboard the moored vessel and secure all the lines in a matter of a few seconds.

Instead, at the final approach, the vessel leaped ahead at the wrong instant, caroming headlong into the moored ship in a violent, embarrassing crash. The crew from the dockside vessel was thrown from its bunks, dishes in the galley smashed. Harinxma was humiliated—and baffled. What had happened? He ran through the maneuver in his head a thousand times and repeatedly questioned the engineers, who said they had relayed his command exactly as given.

We don't learn the truth until late in the book: one of the engineers, the hapless "Porks," flubbed the order; when he got the order he accidentally pressed the engine controls to full ahead instead of half-astern. He'd made a simple dyslexic error in a close-quarters situation. But Harinxma does not know this and remains haunted by the problem throughout the story. The result was two fold: he would never trust his ship until he found out what the error was, and Porks would never trust himself.

This sort of unease can stem from any number of things, from a psychological maneuvering quirk, as with *Isabel Kwel* and her dyslexic engineer, or from some design feature that doesn't quite reveal itself. But it can also be the result of inexperience—you fumble for the correct action in an exciting moment, when everything seems to be happening at once. This plagues a novice sailor. You feel as though you're three steps (or more) behind whatever it is that's unfolding in front of you. Your mind feels cluttered and sluggish, your hands clumsy and wooden. The sails may be luffing like mad, the boom clattering around noisily overhead, the lines hanging in the water in the most unseamanlike way. With a little experience you'll learn to keep calm, to trim the sails smoothly, turn the tiller so the boat catches the wind again, and return the boat to order. But it's the moments of high excitement that challenge the nerves.

I had a similar sense of unease aboard a schooner that I ran for several years on Casco Bay in Maine. *Bagheera* is seventy-two feet long overall, designed by John Alden and built in East Boothbay, Maine, in 1924. A partner and I had bought her in San Francisco, enjoyed a tremendous adventure getting her "home" to Maine, and then started a schoonering business where none had existed in the decades since sail power had died. From the first moment I walked her decks in a stiff breeze, as we tacked our way out past Angel Island and into the open seaway of the Golden Gate, I felt a vague uneasiness with how she handled. We heeled hard in the fifteen knots of wind, but unlike previous vessels I'd sailed, I didn't sense that there was a point where she would stop heeling, the point at which her heavy keel would resist the force of the wind and keep her upright. Her "tenderness" (how much and how quickly she heeled) seemed to continue much past the usual 10 or 15 degrees. In fact, green water would wash over the rails in such a great gust that she would be pressed onto her beam ends in an instant. It was a disconcerting feeling—not knowing when—*if*—she would stabilize or just keep rolling. Since her captain and owner seemed perfectly at ease, I chalked it up to my own lack of familiarity with sailing smaller schooners; most of my experience was on boats closer to 100 feet in length and weighing some 100 tons.

This issue never went away as long as I sailed her. For three years, when the weather report called for fifteen knots of wind or more, especially if it was calling for strong gusts, I would have a knot in my stomach as we headed out with a load of passengers (even with two reefs in the mainsail). There were several spots in the harbor where I knew the wind had a way of popping out in cannon-like bursts, a slot that was reminiscent of those first hours on San Francisco Bay. And a few times, perhaps a half dozen, we would be caught by a gust that would heel us over so far that passengers would be caught up to their waists in green water, scrambling in panic for the high rail, before I could head the boat into the wind and ease the pressure of the wind on her sails.

In *Bagheera*'s case it was a design flaw, at least, a flaw in a feature that had been added to her design many years after she was launched. In the 1940s, according to the history we'd been able to piece together, she had had her gaff rig converted to a Bermuda (or Marconi) rig, perhaps for ease of handling by a smaller crew. This taller rig meant that more sail area was higher up in the rig so that when she heeled, less wind spilled over the top of the rig. Or, conversely, she would be more inclined to be pinned over on her beam ends because of the additional sail area added up high. It wasn't until after I sold the business to my partner and he had the boat reverted to its original gaff rig that I would learn the secret. Sailing under the new gaff rig, there was none of that mysterious, disconcerting tenderness. When she heeled, she stopped at a certain angle and wouldn't go further, regardless of how hard the gusts were. The excess wind simply spilled over the top of the rig because of the reduced height of the gaff sails. The passengers sipped their wine with the same relaxed manner they had imagined when musing at the pretty pictures in the brochure. John Alden must have known this, of course, which is why he drew the boat with a gaff rig, but you couldn't have figured out the potential problem without the experience of sailing the boat with a Marconi rig. It was a tremendous relief to me (*I wasn't crazy*), albeit one that came too late for my tenure with her.

This is an excellent example of what Howard Chapelle cautioned against in *American Small Sailing Craft*: the boats in his book "are unities in hull and rig. They were thoroughly tested in the field of their operation by critical and competitive means. Therefore, the experienced designer, builder, or owner should hesitate to improve upon them until he has had actual experience with the original." (Sound advice for most things in life, actually.)

Block and Tackle

Block and tackle are, in landsman's parlance, pulley and rope. Together, the blocks (pulleys) and line combine to increase pulling strength. Inside a block is a sheave, the turning steel wheel with ball bearings that rotate around the pin. With every sheave you add after the first one, you increase pulling strength proportionately. A single block offers no mechanical advantage; it simply changes the direction of force. By adding a second block, though, you've doubled your pulling power or cut the weight in half. Add another and you decrease the pulling effort by one-third. And so on.

Block and tackle ——

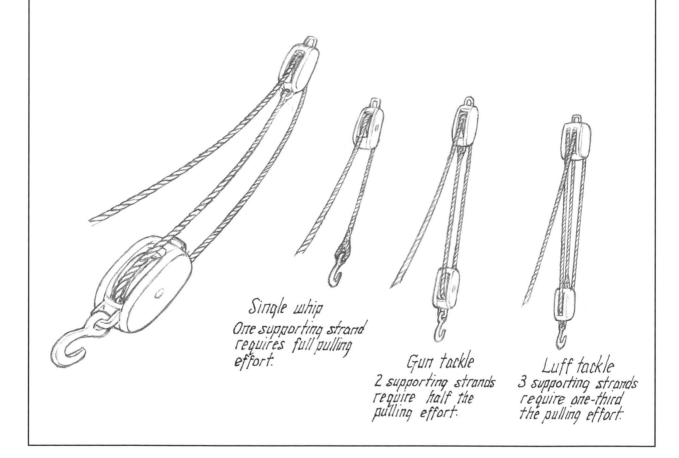

Single whip
One supporting strand requires full pulling effort.

Gun tackle
2 supporting strands require half the pulling effort.

Luff tackle
3 supporting strands require one-third the pulling effort.

The capacity to operate a boat has nothing to do with one's ability to name the various parts on it. A solitary American could competently sail a French boat in Greek waters as comfortably as a Russian could sail a Japanese boat in Australian waters. And the opposite is true, too: if you knew the proper name of every part of the boat—in six different languages—but had never sailed on one, you would be lost and helpless attempting to set sail and find your way out of the harbor for the first time. Once you know your way around a boat, you develop judgment for the function of various bits of hardware and the running rigging—all the lengths of line that serve to trim the sails. You sense a boat's stability and safety because it fits within your experience of how other boats performed. Following is an overview of the various parts of boats, offered not because there will be a test but because there will come a time when your learning curve will be ready for such information. But don't let it get in the way of simply going sailing.

DAGGERBOARDS, CENTERBOARDS, AND KEELS

When a sailboat moves through the water under sail, it is actually being *pulled*, diagonally, by the lift created on the backside of the sails (called the "luff" of the sail). Moving through the water downwind, that is, with the direction of the wind "abaft the beam" (from a direction that is behind the beamiest (widest) section of the vessel), the boat will move fairly easily in the direction it is steered by the tiller. But to steer closer to the wind, with the wind forward of the beam, one needs something to resist the sideslip—to straighten the pull of the wind on the sails into an upwind course. This feature can be a deep keel, a centerboard, a daggerboard, or a set of leeboards.

Howard Chapelle, that great historian of American nautical arcana, credits the invention of the center- and daggerboard to numerous cultures throughout history. He gives credit for development of center- and daggerboards variously to the Chinese, the ancient Formosans (Taiwanese), and several tribes of South American Indians who slipped daggerboards between the hulls of their bamboo and balsa boats. The centerboard as we know it was supposedly invented by a British naval officer, a fellow described only as Shuldham, in 1809—but then largely ignored by British naval architects.

Not until the 1850s did the Americans seize on this innovation and exploit its full capacity for its burgeoning fleet of coastal sailing vessels. Europeans had been using leeboards for centuries. Leeboards, which, while handy enough in practice, look like a garage inventor's answer to countering sideslip; they are ugly and clumsy looking. When sailing upwind, the board on the windward side is raised, while the board on the lee side is left in place—thus the name. L. Francis Herreshoff, in *The Compleat Cruiser*, delights in telling of the functional joys of leeboards. (Indeed, several of Herreshoff's designs reflected this love of leeboards.) In a chapter that takes place on Nantucket,

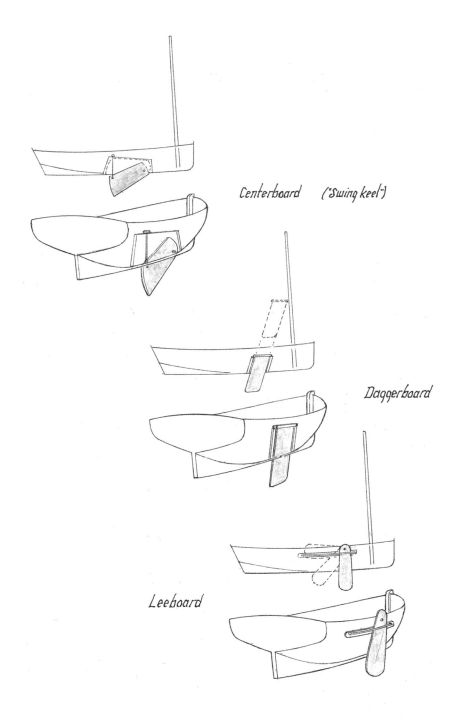

Centerboard   ("Swing keel")

Daggerboard

Leeboard

—— Drop-keel options for a sailing dinghy ——

Herreshoff's protagonists meet the crew of *Tranquilo*, a gaff-rigged ketch with lee-boards. "The lee boards are not as much bother as you might think," says Brewster, the boat's owner. "In short tacking, like sailing up a harbor, we leave them both down. It is only on long hitches that the weather [windward] board is raised."

Even on pretty vessels, leeboards look jerry-rigged, as though two sheets of plywood were scabbed in place on the sides of the boat. It's no wonder American sailors of the early 19th century took one look at the awkward Dutch and French coastal craft and thought, "There's got to be a better way."

The better way was clearly with centerboards (and later, with smaller vessels, daggerboards). While leeboards swing into place outside the hull, along each side, daggerboards and centerboards slip into place on the centerline. Centerboards, also called swing keels, particularly in the American South, swing into place on a pivot, controlled by a cable or rope on deck. Daggerboards, which are typically found on smaller craft such as Lasers and Sunfish because they become too heavy to manipulate on larger vessels, are pushed straight into place so that they extend several feet below the keel. The genius of these innovations is evident in two ways: you immediately solve the problem of slipping sideways through the water under sail, but you also can scoot through shallow water, or even right up on a beach, when they are raised. In the United States in the 19th century, oystermen and other shallows fishermen soon came up with a fleet-footed design called the sharpie, which drew practically no water with the centerboard up and could wriggle around in the shallow estuaries of America's East Coast bays.

There are drawbacks to centerboards, of course. With leeboards, you can see all the moving parts and keep an eye on them for wear and tear. With centerboards, the connection between the lifting cable is hidden by the centerboard trunk. Theoretically, one should endeavor to inspect one's hardware at least once a year, but inspecting the inside of your centerboard trunk or its fussy little fastenings that are hidden in tiny places is most often ignored by just about everyone I know. It's too easy to ignore. So the result is that you forget all about the little shackle holding the centerboard cable in place until it corrodes, the cable comes off in your hand, and the centerboard remains deployed, hanging limply beneath the boat, unable to be retracted. Worse, the pivot itself—a simple bolt or pin that holds the centerboard in place—can corrode, and so the centerboard simply drops to the bottom like a knife, gone forever. I know at least one schooner captain who lost his centerboard in the middle of Penobscot Bay in Maine.

This calls to mind the basic tenet involving knowing your boat: if you can't lay your hand on every piece of hardware on your boat in a regular way (once a week, once a month, once a year—whatever makes sense), you're not practicing safe seamanship.

Natural processes, particularly in the marine environment, have a way of sneaking up on you: corroding steel (even stainless), degrading fabric, rotting wood, and eating away at bronze.

Herreshoff's Mr. Brewster goes on to explain his affection for leeboards and his antipathy toward centerboards in a bellicose diatribe. Centerboard slots tend to get jammed with sand and rocks when the boat is run ashore, the centerboard trunk takes up too much space inside the cabin, and building centerboard trunks is tricky and therefore costly. But that's the great thing about boat design. For every devotee of a certain clever design feature, there is someone else who abhors the same feature for reasons that are particular to his or her brand of sailing. Most of Herreshoff's characters take on a preachy tone when holding forth on their sailing preferences. If anyone does this in real life, it's time to break for the exits when it comes to boat design.

An added benefit to centerboards (and leeboards, for that matter) is their tendency to act as unintended depth-sounders. When you're sailing along and you suddenly feel a most-unseamanlike *bumpity-bumpity-bumpity* you have likely touched the bottom with your centerboard. If you hit a rock squarely, you likely haven't done any damage other than to ding the leading edge of the centerboard. It will simply swing up, out of the way. You can bend a centerboard if you touch bottom at an angle, but this is pretty unlikely. Touching bottom is bound to happen in your seagoing career, and doing so with a centerboard is far preferable to driving hard aground with a full keel. If your centerboard does bounce along the bottom, it's your cue to pull it up the rest of the way and sail off (somewhat sheepishly, perhaps) in the other direction. Sailors of full-keel boats don't have that luxury.

A few final words on centerboards bear mentioning. Centerboard trunks tend to leak, particularly if made of wood. (The trunk, or case, is what houses the centerboard inside the boat.) This is because the builder has deliberately built into the boat a section that simply cannot be maintained and therefore violates the basic tenet of seamanship outlined above (find a way to lay your hands on every piece of the boat regularly). You may be able to inspect a centerboard trunk, at least from the outside when the boat is out of the water, but you really can't get inside it to caulk and paint. "No matter how heavy and strong a centerboard case is built, the shrinking and swelling of the boards at the side of the case cause leaks at the forward and after ends of the box," Herreshoff's Mr. Brewster said. But if the builder did a good job, coating the materials with all manner of toxic-rot inhibitors and sealing the seams with 3M's

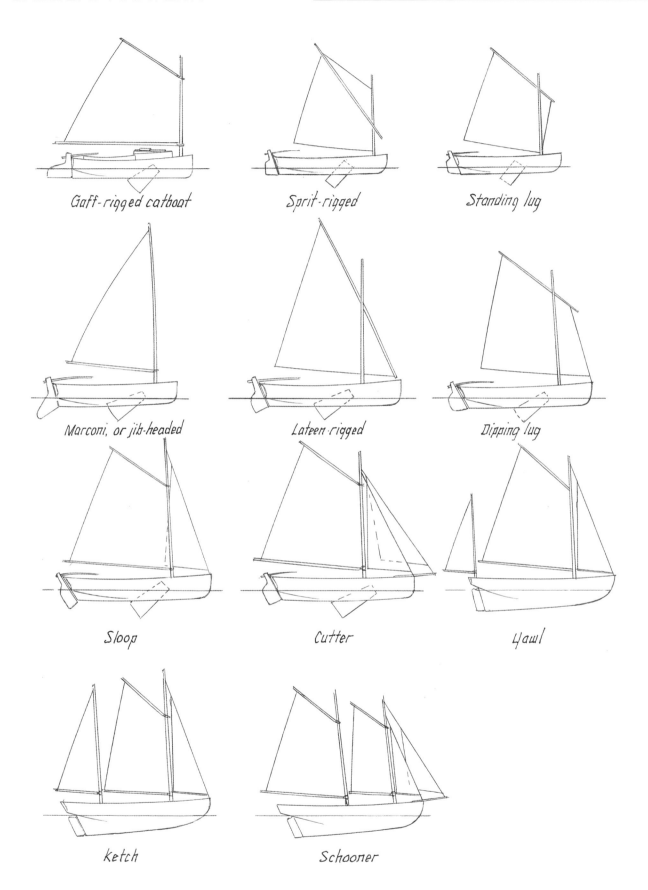

Gaff-rigged catboat

Sprit-rigged

Standing lug

Marconi, or jib-headed

Lateen-rigged

Dipping lug

Sloop

Cutter

Yawl

Ketch

Schooner

finest marine glue, you'll get years of enjoyment out of the boat. But it will still likely leak. This basic fact prompted Howard Chapelle to postulate that this was one reason why centerboards were slow to catch on, despite their practicality. Building a leak-proof centerboard trunk was simply too expensive for New England boatbuilders and not worth fiddling with until "competition forced them to."

You can be at peace with this, though, resting assured that every other centerboard trunk in the world is leaking, too. Just keep an eye on it; if the leak increases, you may have a growing problem that warrants a shipwright's attention. Otherwise, keep sailing your centerboard boat in the shallow bays and harbors that sailors with full keels can only dream of.

Fixed keels, as discussed, stay where they are. There are numerous designs these days, from the traditional lead or steel keel affixed to the underside of the hull with keel bolts, to deep-fin keels with bulbs on the ends. Our model boat, *Swallow*, has a deep keel with outside ballast, meaning the lead is secured with keel bolts up through the wooden keel. Some boats, although very few these days, are fitted with inside ballast—stones, steel ingots, or lead pigs—which enables the sailor to have shallow draft but still enjoy the stiffness of a full-keel boat. This is a compromise, since inside ballast tends to shift on rough days, you can't keep the bilges cleaned and well inspected unless you unload the ballast at the end of each season, and grounding such a boat can cause major structural problems. One of Herreshoff's cruising characters explains this issue thus: "I remember very well going through Canapitsit Channel between Cuttyhawk [Cuttyhunk] and Nashawena Island in Buzzard's Bay many years ago. We were on a heavily built vessel with all inside ballast. She only touched bottom slightly or rubbed over a smooth ledge which is there. This grounding caused hardly a perceptible quiver on deck but apparently the garboards were started"—the bottommost planks jolted loose—"for she at once began to leak."

But with a fixed keel with outside ballast, a boat can withstand quite a drubbing, even from a heavy swell, since the weight is outside the boat and not threatening to pound its way through the planking.

My friend Steve Major keeps a small Friendship sloop moored in Friendship, Maine. It is only twenty-two feet long, a mere slip of a vessel. But it has a deep keel and a broad cockpit typical of these designs, which were working boats of the 19th century that utilized the large cockpits for managing fishing gear and the deep keels for their stability in working in heavy swells. Major, a large-animal veterinarian based in New Hampshire, is a bit of a polymath. He keeps draft horses, he runs a sugarhouse, and all his sap (and

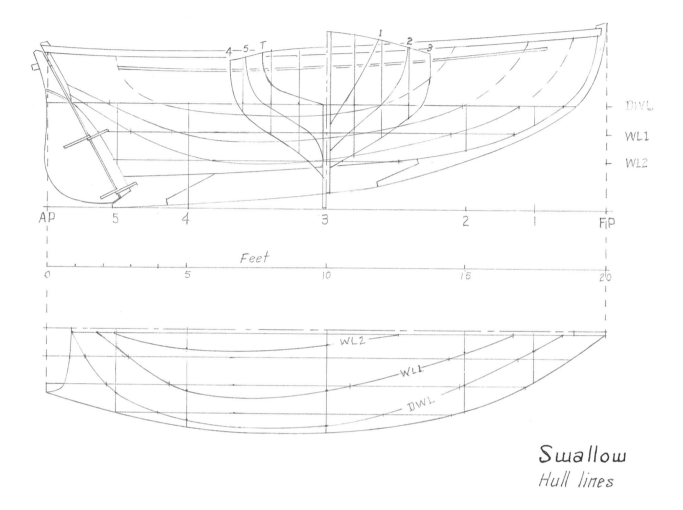

Swallow
Hull lines

firewood for the evaporator) is brought to the house on a heavy sled that the horses pull through the woods and fields near his house in southern New Hampshire.

Major likes to combine his passions. Every year, after boiling off his sap and making about 100 gallons of syrup, he bottles up a load of syrup and drives to Friendship in his pickup truck, where he loads the precious cargo in his sloop. He then heads offshore for the rockbound island of Monhegan—twelve miles distant, not even visible from the coast until he's several miles out. On a day when the wind is blowing freshly from the Northwest, he can make the trip in just a couple of hours, soaring along with the large mainsail wung-out and carving his way through the swells like a small but heavy locomotive. On a bad day, when the wind is southeast, it might take him all day to punch through the opposing wind and seas, getting a good thrashing for his trouble.

Major then pulls his sloop alongside the seawall on Monhegan's little waterfront and unloads the syrup, which is destined for the two inns on the island, The Monhegan House and The Island Inn. This is their syrup for the summer tourist season. Major

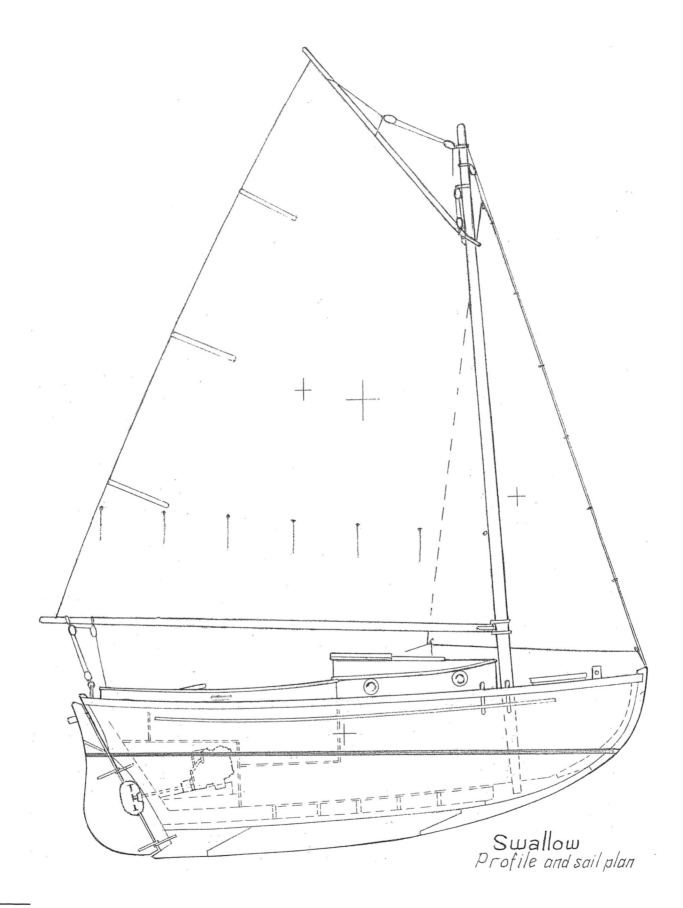

Swallow
Profile and sail plan

performs what may be the world's only sail-powered delivery of maple syrup that was produced by the power of two draft horses.

This delivery would not be possible in a small, light-displacement centerboard sloop. It is only because of the deep keel and full shape of the hull that he can charge offshore in all weather and deliver his cargo. There's nothing like a planing hull for speed—you skim the waves like a skua hunting prey. You can feel this difference when you sail a full-keeled boat as you lumber along, more a part of the waves than something skimming the surface.

There's a cultural divide here: those who yearn for speed above all else, and those who see sailing as a part of seamanship as a whole. Speed might be one part of it. Everyone loves caroming along in a fresh breeze. But safety and comfort are just as compelling. Needless to say, around-the-world yacht races today, the America's Cup and the numerous high-budget speed frenzies, involving budgets that are many millions of dollars, have no time for displacement boats; they're simply too slow. Displacement hulls are the province of retro-types in the molds of celebrated circum-navigators of the last century, beginning with Joshua Slocum in *Spray* and carried on by Bernard Moitessier, Sir Francis Chichester, and Sir Robin Knox-Johnston. Today, the full-keeled displacement mantle is carried by Canadians Lin and Larry Pardey, who have lived aboard their gaff-rigged cutter *Taleisin* for decades.

"If you're going to enjoy sailing and cruising, don't have a schedule," Lin Pardey said after receiving the Cruising Club of America's Far Horizon Award for their lifetime contribution to the sport of sailing. "The ocean doesn't believe in schedules."

It's odd to think of a cultural divide along the lines of something as innocuous and perhaps banal as the shape of one's hull. But it's real enough because the differences in hull shapes bring out a vastly different worldview: advocates of planing hulls—those that skim the waves—urge the pursuit of speed above all else. Boats with a light-displacement hull and fitted with fin keels can feel twitchy under your seat, like a race horse at the gate. Their fin keels dig deep in the water, and their narrow keels enable the boats to make sudden turns, making the whole ensemble skittish and lively. In fact, yachtsman Steve Dashew advocates the exact opposite view of the Pardeys, suggesting that a faster boat means being able to avoid rough weather altogether, since you can outrun them in a light-displacement hull.

Meanwhile, devotees of displacement hulls—those that are more a part of the environment than that scoot its surface—say there's more to sailing than the fastest route, such as safety, enjoyment, and a sublime connection to the natural world. There's the

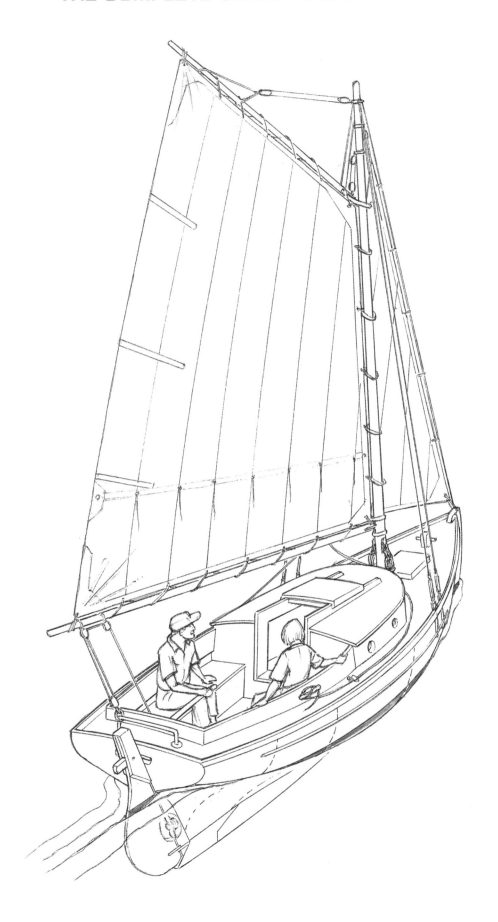

Full keel —

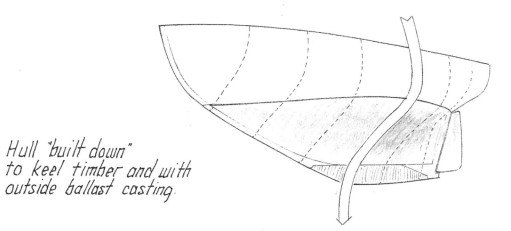

Hull "built down"
to keel timber and with
outside ballast casting.

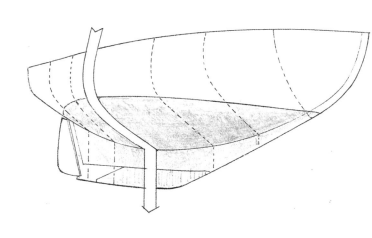

Hull built atop a flat-sided
"skeg" keel with outside ballast.

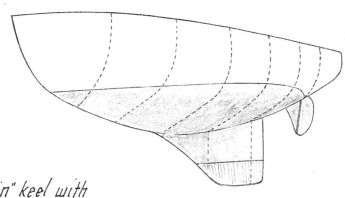

Hull set atop "fin" keel with
independent spade rudder.

Different hull types — for rowing, sailing, or power —

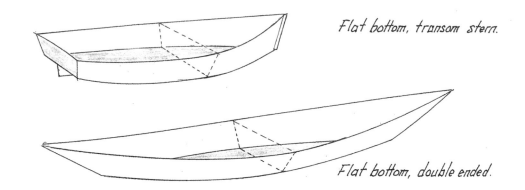

Flat bottom, transom stern.

Flat bottom, double ended.

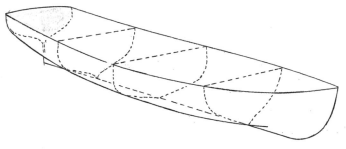

Vee bottom, transom stern, single chine.

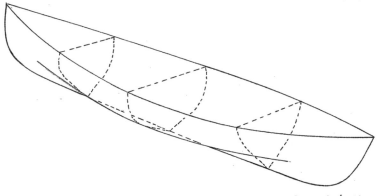

Round bottom, transom stern.

Round bottom, double ended.

same split in surfing: short-boarders are flashy speed freaks, whereas longboarders claim to seek a deeper connection with the wave; they lock into a peeler, settle back on the board's tail or hang ten on the nose, and just *cruise* as long as the wave will carry them.

This is less of an issue for near-coastal sailing, since one can be just as safe in a wave skimmer near shore as in the most overbuilt displacement boat, since land is always right there—easily reachable and a mere call for help away. This is not an option off-shore, of course, where there are fewer boats and a lack of rescue options. This issue comes to the fore every time there's a high-profile rescue of a round-the-world sailor in the inhospitable waters of the Southern Ocean. Displacement types always shave their index fingers in the direction of these capsized speed demons—*tsk, tsk, shouldn't have been going so fast!* And then they suggest that the chagrined sailors be obliged to pay the million-dollar tab for the helicopter rescue. But there is no right way to sail or to gain enjoyment on a sailboat. I go out of my mind when I find myself stuck in a sail-boat race, preferring the leisure of exploring the natural world or allowing my schedule to be dictated by the wind and waves. For others, the thrill of competition maximizes their sailing pleasure.

However, in one parting shot against speed sailors, I offer two examples of the ben-efits of sailing aboard deep-displacement boats, those involving the first person to sail alone around the world, Joshua Slocum, and the first person to sail alone around the world nonstop, Robin Knox-Johnson. *Spray* was a chunky workhorse, built perhaps in the early part of the 19th century as an oyster sloop, lying rotting in a Massachusetts field when Slocum found and subsequently rebuilt it in an apple orchard. When he sailed *Spray* to Rio de Janeiro, she sailed under a simple cutter rig, but then he had her re-rigged with a small jigger back aft, making her a yawl. This balanced the rig with the hull perfectly, such that for the remainder of his voyage he would not have to touch the boat's tiller. He could simply set the sails, trim them to the proper angle for his course, and then lash the tiller in place. In a 2,400-mile voyage between Thursday Island, Australia, to Cocos Keeling, he steered by hand for only three hours, and most of this time was spent tacking into the harbor.

Robin Knox-Johnston remembered this fact when he was sailing alone across the Southern Ocean in 1968, taking part in the Golden Globe Race around the world. His self-steering gear had shattered in the Indian Ocean, but he found, sailing his heavy-displacement *Suhaili*, that he could step away from the cockpit by balancing the rig and lashing the tiller. *Voila!* The boat sailed on its course. (Knox-Johnson went on to win the race and claim his title as the first person to sail alone around the world nonstop.) You simply can't do this with a light-displacement sled. These boats are simply too skittish to muscle their way through the waves with the helm lashed without sensitive self-steering gear such as a servo blade or autopilot. Numerous yacht designers and naval architects have since marveled at Slocum's perfectly-balanced hull and rig and, while they slighted the crude look of *Spray*, had nothing but praise for its effectiveness at sea.

Another handy attribute of the deep-displacement hull is the ease with which you can heave-to in foul weather. Heaving to is the act of aligning the sails and rudder in opposition to one another: the helm goes hard over to starboard, for example, while the jib is backed to starboard and the mainsail sheeted in tight. The force of the wind on the jib attempts to push the bow to port. The rudder, however, counteracts this force, effectively stalling the boat in place. The mainsail tries to drive the boat forward, but the opposing forces of the jib and rudder amount to a back-and-forth scalloping motion that translates into a slow, sideways drift of about half a knot, even in the most horrendous conditions.

Peter Nichols, in his book, *A Voyage for Madmen*, when discussing how Knox-Johnston rode out Southern Ocean storms in *Suhaili*, describes this motion thus:

[An] almost magical component of heaving to is the slick, or wake left by a boat's hull. This is the area of sea immediately to windward, between the boat and the oncoming waves, created by the wind pushing the stalled, resisting boat slowly through the water. The water surface in the boat's wake appears slightly disturbed, like the water on one side of a moored buoy in a strong tidal stream, and almost glassy, like an oil slick. This has the astonishing effect of interrupting the heaping waves as they reach it. Large breaking seas are suddenly tripped by the slick, lose their height and power, and tumble harmlessly before reaching the drifting boat.

This is perhaps the most concise and convincing description of the value of heaving to and also a vivid illustration of the way in which a heavy displacement boat becomes a part of the sea in heavy weather. Its value has been bandied by the Pardeys for decades yet mocked and derided by the speed freaks as retro and old-fashioned. Nichols allows that it's possible to heave a light-displacement boat to, but he doesn't get into particulars. I've never been able to do it in a boat with a fin keel; they're just too fast and twitchy, making the most of every gust to translate the force of the wind into forward speed.

STEERING GEAR: TILLERS AND WHEELS

Tillers are the simplest steering gear—just a lever on a slab of wood that is mounted on pivots at the stern of the boat. You push the tiller over to starboard, say, and, as long as you're making headway through the water, your boat turns to port. And vice versa.

Steering gear ——

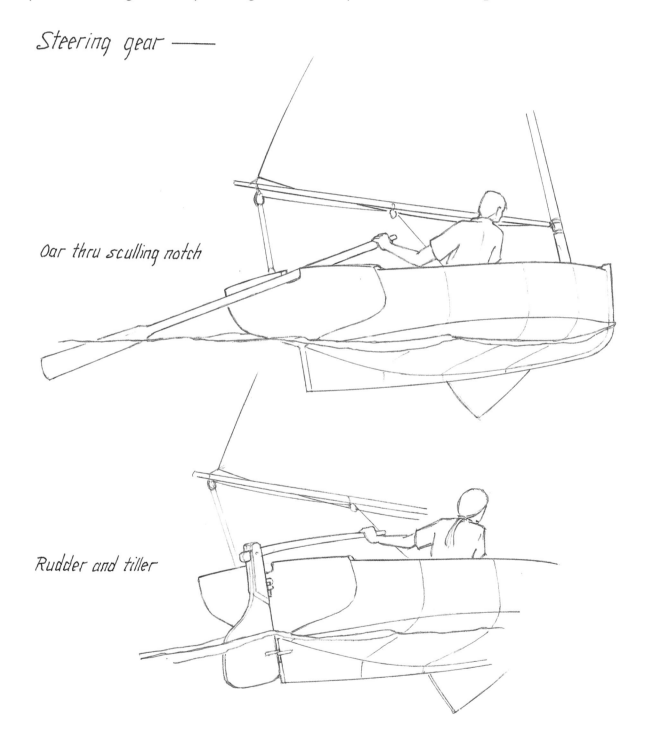

Oar thru sculling notch

Rudder and tiller

Wheel steering systems —

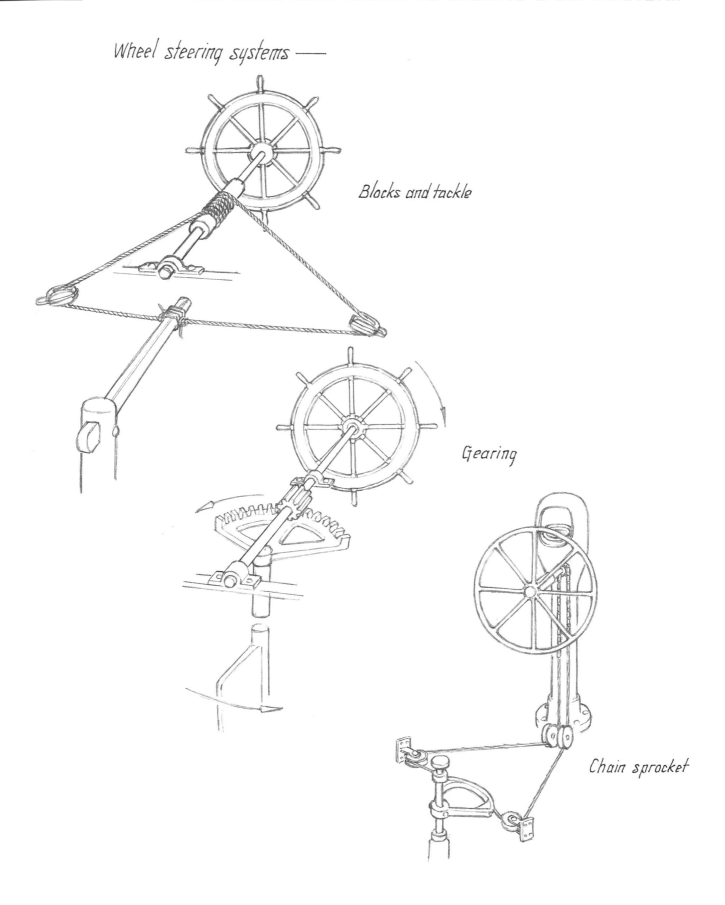

Blocks and tackle

Gearing

Chain sprocket

This can be a little confusing to the beginner. Push the tiller one way and the boat turns the other. But after a few tacks (turning the boat through the wind and sailing off with the sails full on the opposite side), it becomes second nature. A child of five can get it.

Tillers are the easiest steering gear to maintain, since all the gear is right there in front of you, not hidden beneath the deck or in an enclosed pedestal. The technical names for the rudder's mounting hardware—pintle and gudgeon—is even fun to say. Throw those words around at the boatyard and you're bound to raise an eyebrow of respect.

A worm drive is perhaps the most rugged of steering systems. Built of steel, a worm drive functions with one end of a giant screw (also called the pinion or the worm) attached to the helm itself and the other end passing through a grooved quadrant or other gear, which is mounted on the top of the rudder's stock. (Picture the tuning pegs on a guitar.) You can inspect the worm drive by lifting the hatch above the rudder. It should be well lubed with a heavy, waterproof grease. The grease smoothes the action of the gears, but it also keeps away rust. I have always made it a habit to pull off the hatch and inspect the gear before getting underway, turning the helm hard over in one direction and then hard over in the other.

The most common form of yacht steering these days, other than a tiller, involves a set of steel cables turning a quadrant. This is because it can be rigged to a large wheel, giving the helmsman great mechanical advantage. There are drawbacks to this system, most notably, that the system has numerous moving parts that can fail at the worst possible moment. Every offshore seaman has a story of cramming himself into the rear compartment—the lazarette—in storm conditions, trying to reave cable through a sheave that's come adrift. The cable's spurs slice your fingers; your knuckles are skinned as the wrench slips; you bang your head a thousand times.

For coastal sailors, there really isn't a right set of steering gear or a wrong one. It should be easily serviceable and accessible so that it can be kept lubricated and inspected for wear. I once docked a schooner in Portland Harbor in front of a large crowd with a pair of channel-lock pliers serving as the helm, since the helm had come completely loose and was useless in turning the rudder. Earlier in the day, the crew had been varnishing the hatch covers and had removed the helm from the worm gear. When they put it back in place, they hadn't tightened the nut. So I had stepped jauntily aboard, had not checked the steering gear, and, shortly after getting underway, sheered the soft bronze key in the helm's keyway because of the play in the wheel. A thirty-second check of the whole assembly beforehand would have saved me the thrill of that maneuver.

You can't avoid folly in a boat. It lurks everywhere. There is always a hapless Porks malingering belowdecks; there is always a loose cable or unscrewed nut fixing to make its debut of ruining your day. That's life on a boat. Keeping things simple and accessible, though, minimizes the element of surprise.

3

STEERING AND SAILING

"Lift—it must be great stuff; everyone seems to want it. Sailmakers invoke it reverently, naval architects mumble obscure formulas in its name, and even propeller manufacturers will refer to it from time to time."

—from *The Nature of Boats*, by Dave Gerr

This chapter opens with a necessary disclaimer: I am not a racer. In fact, I share L. Francis Herreshoff's ambivalent view of racing as something that is not worth the fuss and detracts from the true enjoyment of spending the day on boats. "I have ten times as much fun in these informal brushes than in any yacht race," commented one of his characters in *The Compleat Cruiser* during an ad hoc race against a cruising friend, "for in the first place you are rid of any frowning regatta committee, or sea lawyers with books full of all the changes in the Vanderbilt Rules. I want to have fun when I go sailing and not be a sadist thinking of luffing, fouls, collisions and disqualification."

Herreshoff's sailors had even agreed, on their informal race from their anchorage at Anisquam, Mass., to Manchester Harbor, that they were allowed to use their engines if they wanted. That's my kind of race!

I should also apologize to my friends who are sailboat racers. I'm sure racing to them is fun—as they fiddle with the topping lifts, the vang, and their weight distribution to eke out every ounce of speed, and squawk at one another about rights of way—but, to me (and L. Francis), it's incredibly stressful and not at all relaxing. This book is about seamanship as much as it is about sailing. In other words, it is not simply about the most efficient and speediest form of getting from one place to another. Therefore, it offers a holistic view of boats rather than a narrow one found in the latest edition of a racing rule book.

This chapter relates information that is perhaps the most difficult for the novice to understand without real-world experience. It deals with the mysterious Bernoulli Principle, various weather vectors related to "lift" and "leeway," and how the sailboat's construction, rig, and steering gear bring it all together in a straight path through the water. And while it's a little abstract to read about three-dimensional forces, it's really not that hard in reality. You just have to go for it.

The mechanics of steering and sailing are simple enough: the surface wind applies force on the sail's foil shape and the keel and rudder redirect that force to move the boat in the desired direction. The trick is understanding how these elements are manipulated—to trim the sails and steer the boat. Diagrams are somewhat necessary to show how these forces work, but, really, experimentation is the path toward understanding.

In his book *First You Have to Row a Little Boat*—a book that is one part sailing manual and one part self-help treatise—Richard Bode contends that you can't begin to appreciate the complexity of sailing without first mastering a small rowing dinghy. There's some truth to that approach: you shouldn't drive a car until you've learned to change a tire or check the oil; just as you can't paint a boat or a house without appreciating how to care for a brush. Or, as Mr. Miagi admonished in *The Karate Kid*, you can't learn karate until you can expertly paint a fence or wax a car: "Wax on, wax off," etc. I learned to sail on large sailing ships, first heading to sea in a 125-foot, steel schooner called *Westward* that was operated by the Sea Education Association (SEA) in Woods Hole, Mass. I had no idea how any of the rig worked when I first stepped aboard as a deckhand; I knew nothing of the wind's effects on the sails. I didn't even know that the wind tended to blow from a single direction at the same time. Rather, I sort of envisioned the wind swirling about—like it does in the corner of a yard in autumn, leaves spiraling on its gusts. So for me it did start with the absolute basics. There was simply

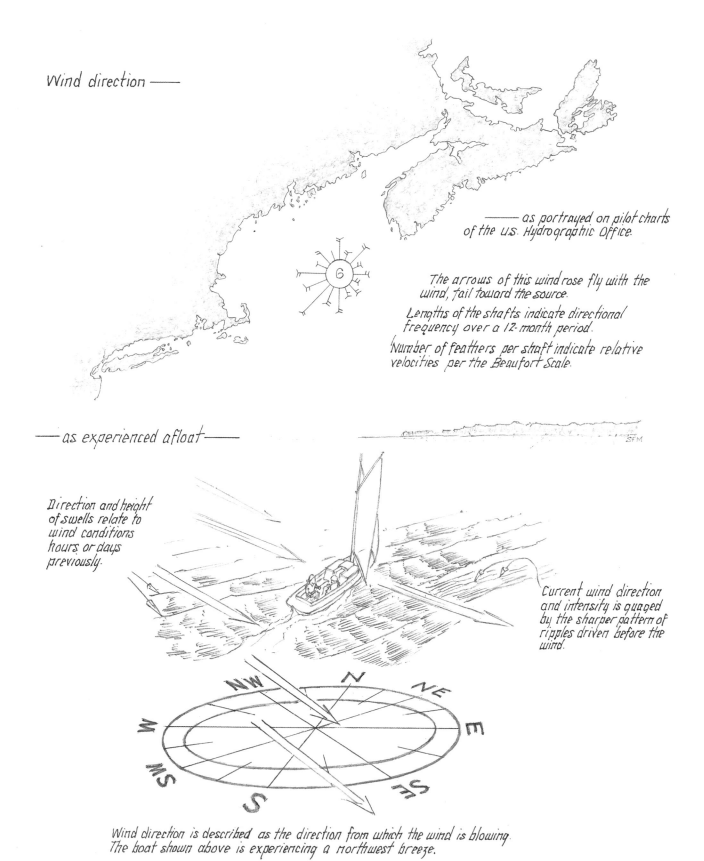

Wind direction ——

—— as portrayed on pilot charts of the U.S. Hydrographic Office.

The arrows of this wind rose fly with the wind, tail toward the source.

Lengths of the shafts indicate directional frequency over a 12-month period.

Number of feathers per shaft indicate relative velocities per the Beaufort Scale.

—— as experienced afloat ——

Direction and height of swells relate to wind conditions hours or days previously.

Current wind direction and intensity is guaged by the sharper pattern of ripples driven before the wind.

Wind direction is described as the direction from which the wind is blowing. The boat shown above is experiencing a northwest breeze.

too much information to understand all at once. I recall simply learning the lines by physically grabbing hold of them and pulling hard, looking aloft to see what affect my tugs had on some part of the rig. By tugging this line *here* it manipulated that end of the spar and sail *there*. The professional crew went about their business, chirping in a kind of folksy, sailorly gibberish, as I clumsily and slowly assembled a visual vocabulary based on cause and effect. Or, as Richard Henry Dana commented on his first few days at sea in *Two Years Before the Mast*: "Unintelligible orders were so rapidly given and so immediately executed; there was such a hurrying about, and such an intermingling of strange cries and stranger actions, that I was completely bewildered." Through seasickness, beatings, and depravation (or, in Winston Churchill's case, "rum, sodomy, and the lash"), Dana soon learned his way around the deck of the brig *Pilgrim*. For me, it was more mental anguish.

So let's start with the wind. As we all know, the forecast tells us from which direction the wind is predicted to blow and how strong. This is the unobstructed wind, of course. On land, it does blow around buildings and swirl in unpredictable ways. It caroms up and down hills and valleys, dividing around mountainsides and slamming against cliffs. But at sea it really does blow in one direction, since there's nothing there to obstruct its flow. As Nathaniel Bowditch quipped in *American Practical Navigator*, "Wind is air in approximately horizontal motion." You can even read the pattern of its flow on the surface of the waves. Little zephyrs cause riffles on a smooth sea; stronger winds blowing unobstructed over the sea generate enormous waves. In 1805, just a year after Bowditch released his book, an Englishman named Francis Beaufort developed a system that allowed sailors to not only tell the direction of the wind by studying the surface of the sea but actually how strong it was blowing. We call this system the Beaufort Scale, and it's just about the handiest thing there is to reading the force of the wind since it does not require a finicky tool like an anemometer. You look at the surface of the waves, compare it to a set of drawings or photos arranged on a scale from 1 to 12, and judge the safety of the day's sail accordingly.

One thing that's important to remember about the Beaufort Scale is the concept of "fetch." Fetch is the distance over which wind is allowed to blow without obstruction. A true Beaufort Scale is based on unlimited fetch, or open-ocean conditions. So if you're in a protected bay, the waves will never reach the full height listed on the Beaufort Scale, no matter how hard the wind blows. There's just not enough searoom to allow them to build. A hurricane blowing over a mud puddle is still a hurricane, but you won't get

Beaufort Scale of Wind Forces

Beaufort number	Knots per hour velocity	Seaman's description of wind	Mode of estimating for full-rigged ship	Wave pattern	
0	Less than 1	Calm	Full-rigged ship, all sails set, no headway.		Glassy ripples
1	1 to 3	Light air	Just sufficient to give steerage way.		Ripples like fish scales
2	4 to 6	Slight breeze	Speed of 1 or 2 knots, full-and-by (closehauled)		Wavelets without crests
3	7 to 10	Gentle breeze	Speed of 3 or 4 knots		Wavelets atop swells
4	11 to 16	Moderate breeze	Speed of 5 to 6 knots closehauled.		Wavelets lengthening. Occasional whitecaps.
5	17 to 21	Fresh breeze	All plain sail, closehauled.		Waves to 6'. Increased whitecaps.
6	22 to 27	Strong breeze	Ship, closehauled, can just carry topgallant sails.		Waves to 10'. Regular whitecaps.
7	28 to 32	Moderate gale (high wind)	Ship, closehauled, can just carry whole upper topsails.		Breaking waves to 14'. Foam driven downwind.
8	34 to 40	Fresh gale	Ship, closehauled, can just carry reefed upper topsails and whole foresail.		Waves to 18'. Lengthened valleys. Foam streaks downwind
9	41 to 47	Strong gale	Ship, closehauled, can just carry lower topsails and reefed foresail.		Waves to 23'. Crests rolling over. Dense foam streaks.
10	48 to 55	Whole gale (heavy gale)	Ship, closehauled, can only carry main lower topsail.		Waves to 30'. Tumbling crests. Foam everywhere.
11	56 to 65	Violent Storm	Ship can only carry storm staysail or trysail.		Waves to 37'. Wave crests blown to froth.
12	Above 65	Hurricane	No canvas can stand.		Waves to 46'. Visibility affected by spray and foam.

American Merchant Seaman's Manual —1942—

Why a sail pulls to windward ——

Lift of an airplane wing and windward ability of a close-hauled sail
are explained by Bernoulli's Law:

"Where speed is small, pressure is great.
Where speed is great, pressure is small".
(resulting in a partial vacuum or suction zone)

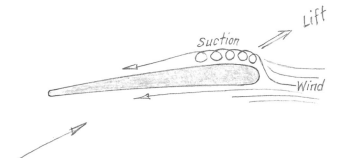

Lift

Suction

Wind

The solid airplane wing moving
forward divides the standing air
into a static stream passing under
and partially supporting the straight
underside, and a rapid stream
climbing the curved upper side
to close again in the wake.

The greater speed of air traveling over the upper side
causes reduction of air pressure over the wing and
an upward suction of air rushing to fill that partial
vacuum.

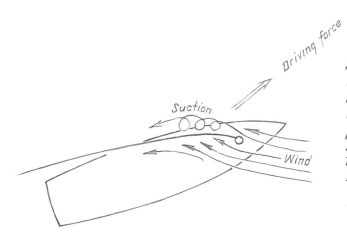

Driving force

Suction

Wind

A close-hauled boat's sail
becomes an airfoil similar to
an airplane wing as wind-blown
air travels a longer and faster
path around the bulging leeward
side, causing a drop in pressure
that sucks the sail and the boat
to windward.

more than rough wavelets on the surface. In other words, the wind blows just as hard
but you couldn't guess it from looking at the water without there being adequate fetch.

Now that we know how to gauge a wind's force—by reading the sea's surface—let's
discuss its direction. On a chart, direction is indicated by a "wind rose." This is basically

a compass drawn onto the chart, showing both magnetic and true direction (more on this later in Chapter 5). Weather forecasts describe the direction *from which* the wind is blowing. For example, a southerly wind blows from the south.

We can't sail directly into the wind, however. To get the boat to move, we adjust—trim—the sail at an angle to the wind so that its shape becomes an asymmetrical foil. The wind on the back side, or "luff," of the sail creates a pressure vacuum, thereby creating lift. Lift *pulls* on the luff of the sail, essentially dragging the boat forward at an approximately 90-degree angle from the direction of the wind. This phenomenon was first discovered by Daniel Bernoulli, an 18th-century Swiss mathematician. (He was also first to coin the term "hydrodynamics," which he used to describe his chosen field.) As the speed of a fluid, liquid, or gas *decreases* the pressure around it actually *increases*. This is the same principle at work on an airplane wing. Gunning your engines in a plane as it speeds down a runway forces air over the wing, and lift is created in a 90-degree angle, propelling the plane upward. Turn this wing shape on its side and you have a sail. The only difference is we're not using the engine as an artificial boost; we're using the given force (and direction) of the wind. Lift is best observed with a single sheet of paper, as detailed in Carl Chase's excellent book, *An Introduction to Nautical Science*. "[H]old a sheet of paper to your chin, just below your lower lip, and blow over the top of it. The paper will rise. It rises because, when you blow, the pressure in the moving stream of air drops to less than the pressure of the still air under the paper. This pressure difference is felt by the paper as a force which pushes it upward."

Lift, as Chase points out, is not to be confused with drag. Drag is simply a clumsy downwind force—like what happens when you blow on a ping-pong ball. A sailboat is capable of moving by this force, too; when it's on a downwind reach it's simply being pushed, not pulled, along on its course. Anything that floats, a log, a beachball, or an oil tanker, is capable of being pushed downwind. But it takes an asymmetrical foil to be *pulled* by the wind.

Now, a boat without a keel or rudder would simply slip sideways just as a plane without flaps would just keep rising. The keel, like the flaps, redirects that force into a straight line, the boat's "course," and the rudder allows the helmsman to fine-tune the "heading" of the boat. Course describes a boat's forward motion, while heading describes the direction the boat is facing at any given time. For example, an inefficiently trimmed sailboat might be heading too close to the wind and therefore making quite a bit of leeway, while its course—the true direction the boat is making through the water—might be 20

Making boats go: Sail, keel and rudder working together.

Rig balance —
A rudderless sailboat has much in common with the swinging arrow of a weathervane.

Wind

A weather vane pivots on a supporting staff. With tail feathers much broader than the point, it swings so as to point directly into the wind.

The sailboat's hull swings on an axis called the Center of Lateral Plane, or Center of Resistance. This center is the location along the hull at which the boat could be dragged sideways if a rope were attached to that spot and pulled.

This pivot point or resistance center can be moved forward or aft by re-shaping the underwater profile during the design stage of a keel boat, or by slanting the centerboard forward or aft in a centerboarder.

or 30 degrees different. A skilled sailor finds that sweet spot, where the boat is heading as close to the wind as possible without suffering undue leeway. To do otherwise—to sail too close to the wind so as to be inefficient—is called "pinching." Pinching, which will earn the helmsman the derisive moniker "dirt farmer" if done too often, is deceptively easy to do: the sails look full and drawing but the speed through the water is disproportionately lower than if the helmsman "fell off" the wind a few degrees.

Our *Swallow* is fitted with a full keel, which runs the length of the hull. The keel's "center of lateral resistance" is the point at which the hull pivots. Or, in the case of a centerboard boat, the pivot point is the centerboard itself. Without that board hanging down, the boat slips effortlessly sideways. With a keel or centerboard in place, it suddenly has a point to swivel around, much like a weathervane. Picture a giant finger pushing against a hull underwater: too far forward and the boat's bow will swing away, too far aft and the stern swings. The point at which this force is balanced is the center of lateral resistance, and, while it's not necessary to empirically know exactly where on your hull that spot is, you want to know that it exists and that it's down there somewhere.

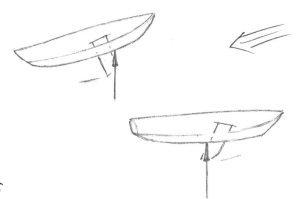

The pivot point moves forward if the centerboard is slanted forward, sending the boat's head higher into the wind.

It moves aft as the centerboard is raked aft, causing the rudderless boat to fall away from the wind.

The same can be said of a sail. Each sail has a "center of effort." It's the point at which all of the sail's pulling power is focused and is a simple math problem if you know the dimensions of your sail. Draw a line from each corner of the sail to the center of the opposite edge of the sail and where these three lines intersect is the sail's center of effort. And if you have more than one sail on a boat, as *Swallow* does, you simply bisect the distance between the sails' two centers of effort to come up with the boat's one center of effort.

A well-balanced boat will have its center of effort and center of lateral resistance perfectly aligned, one over the other. Hypothetically, in a calm sea and in a steady breeze, such a boat will sail indefinitely on a steady course. *Swallow* is such a boat; its rig and hull are mathematically balanced. In reality, however, waves slap against the bow, helmsmen lack perfect concentration, breezes vary in intensity, and the result is that the boat's course wobbles around. So you have to stand at the tiller and steer, heading into the wind when you get a lifting gust and falling off the wind when the boat is headed. Yet a well-balanced rig is a joy to feel—the boat *wants* to sail in the direction it's pointed!

Supposedly Joshua Slocum's *Spray* was such a boat, too. On May 5, 1896, he sailed from Juan Fernandez Island in the South Pacific and, after hanging a left around St. Felix Island, rode the trades and arrived in the Marquesas forty-three days later. "I sailed with a free wind day after day," he wrote. "For one whole month my vessel held her course

If the shape of the underbody determines the pivot point of a boat under sail, then it is the size and location of sails along the hull that causes a sailboat to swing toward, or away from the wind, in the manner of a weathervane, if not checked by the rudder.

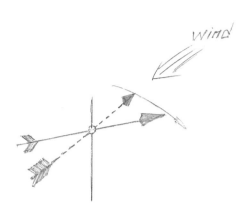

Take away feathers from the tail, or add size to the point, and the vane begins to swing away from the wind.

Close-hauled mainsail reduced by reefing. Full jib retained. The boat cannot lay so closely to the wind as when balanced with her full sail area.

true; I had not, the while, so much as a light in the binnacle. The Southern Cross I saw every night abeam. The sun every morning came up astern; every evening it went down ahead. I wished for no other compass to guide me, for these were true." He had not touched the tiller at all—slept soundly through the night and, during the day, "read my books, mended my clothes, or cooked my meals and ate them in peace."

There's another theory that seeks to explain why a foil shape is so effective at providing motion to sailboats, airplanes, and seagulls. Circulation Lift Theory suggests that there is no low-pressure system lifting a foil because the air on the backside of the foil must travel faster to meet itself on the after edge (leach of the sail). Rather, the foil shape disrupts the flow of air to create a reactive force that—without resistance—forces the object (the sail and boat together) out of the way in the direction of lift, roughly 45 degrees from centerline or perpendicular to the angle of the luff. But both theories are a little like Freudian ones; they sound plausible and are impossible to disprove, therefore, they must be right. But, when it relates to sailboats, who cares? The point is that the forces—whatever they are—provide lift and drive a boat and a plane and a seagull in a predictable vector relative to the angle of the wind.

Rig balance cont'd —

With mainsail raised and loosely sheeted, a rudderless sailboat will drift sideways, swinging on her pivot point until the sail fills and moves her forward in a downwind arc. How quickly she stops, sails shaking, depends on the amount of sail area (the windvane's tailfeathers) abaft the pivot point.

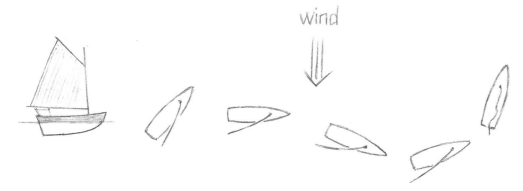

Sail area set entirely ahead of the hull's pivot point will cause a long jog downwind before the boat rounds up.

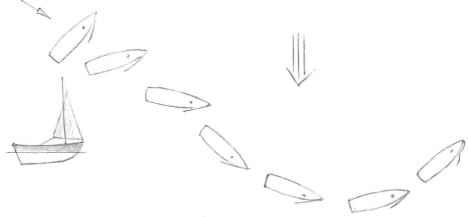

Closehauled, the rudderless sailboat makes a tight arc. This is the heave-to position.

A rudderless sailboat can often be steered by careful sheeting-in, or by loosing sails forward or aft, in the mode of adding or subtracting either arrow-point or tail feathers to direct the posture of a windvane.

A rudderless small boat can often be steered by moving crew weight forward or aft to modify the pivot point location, or by specifically loading-down the bow on one side or the other to cause its increased underwater curve to force the boat's head toward the unweighted side.

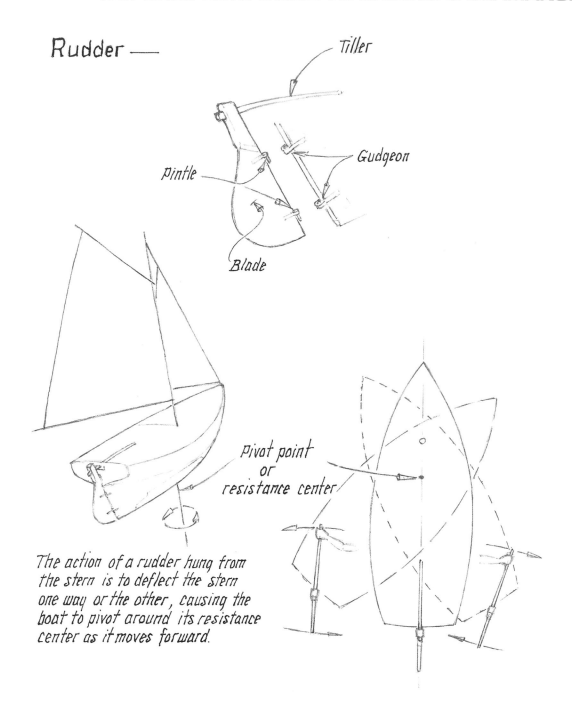

Rudder —

Tiller

Gudgeon

Pintle

Blade

Pivot point
or
resistance center

The action of a rudder hung from
the stern is to deflect the stern
one way or the other, causing the
boat to pivot around its resistance
center as it moves forward.

The above description considers the harmony between rig and keel with all sails set. However, on most boats you can reduce sail—"reef"—to accommodate strong winds. This affects the balance of the rig. If you reduce the size of the mainsail but not the jib, for example, the center of effort, therefore, moves forward on the boat because you have less sail area (less force) applied toward the rear of the craft. Or, by raising one sail and not the other, you have a more dramatic example of this phenomenon. Raising the mainsail and not the jib will cause the boat to pivot into the wind. The mainsail acts like a giant weathervane. Only by raising the jib, introducing effort forward of the pivot point, will it begin to balance and be capable of moving on a single course.

The key to all this is the rudder. The rudder actually forces the boat to pivot around the keel or centerboard by forcing the stern one way or the other. The more balanced the rig, the less the helmsman notices a tug on the rudder. Conversely, the less balanced the rig, the harder it is to steer. If the center of effort is too far forward of the center of lateral resistance (pivot point), the helmsman has to struggle with the tiller to keep the boat from heading away from (falling off) the direction of the wind; too far aft and the boat wants to keep pivoting toward (heading up) the direction of the wind.

Now that we know how to balance our boat in relationship with the wind, let's consider having the boat move on a given course. There are three basic "points of sail," the "close reach," "beam reach," and "broad reach."

Whichever point of sail is desired, the way to achieve maximum efficiency in the sails is to orient your boat on its intended heading and then ease out the sails until they luff (flap). Then pull them in again with the sheets so that the sails just barely stop luffing. This is a little tricky the first few times. If you sail too close to the wind and pinch your course, the sails will luff also. So the trick is to sheet the sails in as tightly as they will go, settle on a course that keeps the sails full and the boat moving (without pinching), and then ease the sails gradually until they begin to luff. Bring them back in again ever so little—and that's your sweet spot!

A close reach is perhaps the most vivid and exciting point of sail. You're sailing as close to the wind as possible without pinching, the wind in your face, as the boat works its way upwind. Sailing close hauled is also where the boat's designer and builder earn their reputation as professionals. The boat will either sail closely to the wind—or it won't. Meaning, it's either a thoroughbred or a bit of a pig. Yet, whatever the breed, when the sails are trimmed tightly and the boat is scooting along on a close reach, the boat actually feels as though it is being pulled effortlessly along on its course, almost as though it were on rails and it was being led by the nose by an unseen force.

In October 1966 Sir Francis Chichester was halfway to Australia on his record-setting voyage around the world aboard *Gipsy Moth IV* when he rounded the Cape of Good Hope and entered the Indian Ocean. He spent the morning of October 18 alternately kneading bread and changing sail until, as the sun came out, he popped the bread in the oven and settled on a suitable sail configuration. The breeze was out

Reaching——

*A sailboat is said to be **reaching** when it moves across the wind.*

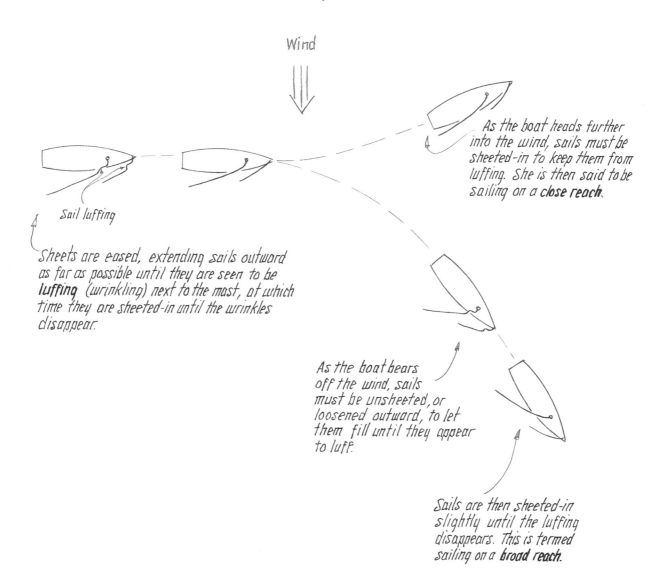

Wind

As the boat heads further into the wind, sails must be sheeted-in to keep them from luffing. She is then said to be sailing on a **close reach**.

Sail luffing

Sheets are eased, extending sails outward as far as possible until they are seen to be **luffing** (wrinkling) next to the mast, at which time they are sheeted-in until the wrinkles disappear.

As the boat bears off the wind, sails must be unsheeted, or loosened outward, to let them fill until they appear to luff.

Sails are then sheeted-in slightly until the luffing disappears. This is termed sailing on a **broad reach**.

of the northeast, parallel to the southeast coast of Africa, and his course was easterly. He was close hauled and feeling on top of the world:

"When all the sails were trimmed *Gipsy Moth* was on a close reach, and went beautifully," he wrote in *Gipsy Moth Circles the World*. "It was pleasant sailing through that sunny afternoon and evening, because the sails and blocks were asleep, and for what seemed the first time for many days my ears were not assailed by the cacophony of barking blocks and cracking sails. The ship sailed as if she were satisfied—to me this is like being on a good horse, riding fast, but within her strength."

A beam reach is when the wind is coming directly over the beam of, or perpendicular to, the vessel. The sails are eased about halfway out. This is a sloppy direction to sail because you are also at greatest risk of rolling mercilessly, since you are also abeam of the seas themselves. Rolling in a beam sea is about the easiest and quickest way to get seasick, and even if you don't get sick you'll be uncomfortable. The boat's motion can be extreme as it rolls back and forth in the troughs and crests of the waves. But if there are not high waves, sailing on a beam reach is pleasant enough, since it does not take the fastidious concentration of sailing close hauled. It's easy to let your mind wander.

And then there's the broad reach, the truly languorous and luxurious point of sail. This is trade wind sailing, the reach of dreamers and idealists. With the sails wung-out almost as far as they will go, the breeze blowing gently over your shoulder, you ease the seat back . . . and just cruise. This is the reach of longboard surfers and the Beach Boys, the direction to sail when you're not of Type A personality, and when you're content to simply see where the wind will take you. Okay, you get the idea. Technically, sailing on a broad reach is simply sailing in what's called a quartering breeze, since it's blowing over the vessel's rear quarter at a slight angle.

Running with the wind is not a reach at all. It is a point of sail, but it's in its own class. You're simply being pushed downwind. It's an ugly way to sail and a potentially dangerous one, too, since the risk of gybe—the sails flying across onto the other tack in an instant—is ever present. Meanwhile, sailing downwind in a moderate or heavy sea also results in an unpleasant corkscrewing motion that is the combination of pitch, yaw, and roll. It's not quite the extreme of rolling in a beam reach, but it's more dangerous if you're not vigilant enough to keep the wind where you want it in relation to the sails. It's easy to get lulled into a false sense of security, too, since there is the illusion of safety. Sailing with the wind, you don't feel much of a breeze on deck. But it's there alright, and if it catches the back of your mainsail, it will send it snapping onto the other tack in a heart-stopping instant, sweeping the deck of any loose limbs or gear with the sails sheets.

Sooner or later, regardless of which point of sail you're on, you're going to have to change course. You will do so in one of two ways, tacking or gybing. Tacking is the most common and simply means turning the boat so that the bow turns toward the direction of the wind, passes through the eye of the wind—sails luffing madly all the while—until you are settled back on the opposite tack on a course that is an equal relative angle to the wind as the one you were on before you tacked.

Tacking — while beating to windward —

⑩ The new tack (now **port tack**) is commenced as the boat makes way to windward.

⑨ Boat straightens up, sails shaking.

⑧ Helm is now put down to commence a tack to starboard.

⑦ This is now **starboard tack** with wind over the starboard side.

⑥ If the tack is made successfully, the sails swing across the boat and settle, still close-hauled, on the opposite (leeward) side. Rudder is brought amidships.

Wind

④ With the helm down the boat comes up into the wind with sails shaking.

⑤ If the tacking maneuver is not successful and the boat hangs in irons with sails flapping amidships, the boat's head can usually be forced through the eye of the wind by **backing** the jib against the wind.

③ Helm is **put down** (tiller pushed to leeward or "down hill") causing the rudder to steer the boat into the eye of the wind in the tacking maneuver.

② Sails are close-hauled or tightened-in to make the boat sail closer to windward without the sails luffing.

① Sailing on a close reach, wind over port side, on **port tack**.

Gybing —while sailing downwind —

Sailing on a broad reach, port tack.

Wind

Sailing downwind — running or scudding — squarely before the wind. Boat is apt to **yaw** one way or the other as her bow is depressed by the wind levering her mast and sails from astern. Crew weight brought aft helps to steady her steering.

Jib and mainsail are hauled inward to gain a midship position prior to a possibly violent filling of the sails from the opposite side.

Mainsail is quietly passed across the boat from its temporary midship position. Wind fills the sails on the now-**starboard** tack. This is a controlled gybe.

In heavy winds, sailing dead-before can result in yawing not controllable by the rudder and ending in a downwind broach or capsize.

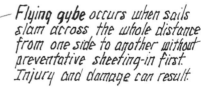

Flying **gybe** occurs when sails slam across the whole distance from one side to another without preventative sheeting-in first. Injury and damage can result.

Controlled gybing — one downwind tack, then the other — can provide a safer downwind course.

This is typically preceded by the sailorly pronouncement, "Ready about!" And then, once everyone onboard has had a moment to prepare for the coming maneuver, you put the helm down and, just as heartily, crow, "Helm's alee!"

On *Swallow*, we would have to cast off the jib sheet on the leeward side of the boat and, once the boat passes "through stays," begin to tighten it up on the opposite side. Some boats have self-tacking jibs, with the jib sheet on a "traveler" that simply scoots from one side of the deck to the other when the boat is tacked. Very handy indeed.

Tacking is exciting, since it is accompanied by a hell of a racket. Sails luff like crazy, blocks rattle, hardware clangs, items down below shift from one side of the boat to the other with a crash—until the tack is complete and you're sailing smoothly along on your new course. This can be terrifying to the uninitiated. To make matters worse, the boat goes from heeling dramatically at one angle, to standing straight up (while the boat loses speed and the sails luff), to heeling at exactly the opposite angle, all in a few short seconds. It's best to give everyone aboard a little more warning than the terse words above.

Gybing involves the same idea—turning the boat so that the sails wind up sheeted on the opposite side of the boat—but the maneuver is vastly different. Instead of turning into the wind, you turn the bow away from it so that the *stern* passes through the eye of the wind. One typically gybes when sailing on a broad reach, since it is a quicker maneuver than rounding all the way around. To tack on a broad reach you would turn the boat roughly 270-degrees to end up on a broad reach on the opposite tack. Whereas gybing from a broad reach would involve only turning the boat roughly 60 degrees.

To gybe takes some modest preparation: bring the mainsail sheets in tight so that the sail is virtually all the way amidships. And then, after calling out, "Prepare to gybe!" to others aboard, turn the tiller or helm so that the stern passes through the eye of the wind. Just as you do so, be sure to keep an eye on the sail. As it snaps across, or just an instant before, shout, "Gybe ho!" The sail will fill; you ease the sheets out and adjust your course until you're sailing along on a broad reach as calmly as you were before the gybe. It's tremendously satisfying.

But to gybe imperfectly, to cause a "flying gybe" or "hot gybe," is to make an ass of yourself. You might damage the rig; you might hurt someone. So take the simple precautions outlined above and people will begin to regard you in the same manner of awe as they might Capt. Jack Sparrow. (Or at least you'll like to think so.)

4

A LOOK AT THE WEATHER

"Mahon said it was a foolish business, and would end badly. I loved the ship more than ever, and wanted awfully to get to Bangkok. To Bangkok!"

—from *Youth*, by Joseph Conrad

Joshua Slocum was about the coolest sailor that ever was. When he set out to sail alone around the world, his onboard equipment was exceedingly simple: a barometer, a taffrail log, tin clock (more about these last two items later), a mess of blocks and tackle, some spare anchors, and a host of simple wood-working and rigging tools that you still find gathering dust in the back corners of nautical antique shops in places like Key West. It's important to remember that he carried no radio, no lifejacket, and nothing that could even be generously considered a liferaft. He stands for the proposition that self-sufficiency at sea is really as simple as the right combination of basic tools and some Yankee ingenuity. Granted, a few years after his solo, round-the-world adventure of 1895-96, he would ultimately be lost at sea. But that fatal adventure came later and likely had very little to do with the point I'm making here: he sailed around the world alone aboard a small boat before it occurred to anyone that it was even possible. He did so safely and with the greatest joy imaginable. Think of Slocum when you consider how much gear you really need to head to sea. What you need is good judgment—judgment about a lot of things—but in this chapter I mean judgment about weather in particular.

Weather, like everything else that you might experience aboard a small boat at sea, happens in context. You do not find yourself at sea in an unknown season at an unknown time on an unknown boat. Instead, you consider the weather conditions and patterns of the previous days, you know your home waters, you know your boat.

The following story is about an adventure I had with a group of friends that brings together many of the lessons that this chapter is intended to illuminate—the context of weather in relationship with the boat and its crew.

The wind built steadily in the early morning hours so that we were making almost eight knots as we sailed past the Buzzard's Bay Light Tower on our approach to the Cape Cod Canal. We were flying along, having completed the crossing from Cape May to Block Island Sound in two nights and a day without incident. We had timed our transit through the Canal perfectly. It was 0645 on the Friday before Memorial Day when we rounded up to strike our sails. The excitement aboard was palpable.

This was the home stretch for a crew of Mainers who had been called upon to rig, launch, and deliver *Bagheera*, a seventy-eight-year-old Alden schooner, from the Sassafras River on Maryland's Eastern Shore back to Maine, where it was built. The voyage actually started in San Francisco, where the boat was hauled out, then put on a truck and delivered to Maryland via Route 80; it was too large to get road permits for crossing New England.

We would be home the following morning, greeted by our beloved, our friends, and a team of newspaper and TV reporters. The media was drummed up by my business partner, who had effectively stoked their interest in this old boat that was coming home. *Bagheera* had been built in East Boothbay, Maine, in 1924, and we were going to use it to launch Portland's only windjammer business, taking passengers on boat rides around Casco Bay.

"She was built in Maine; she's comin' home!" we announced through gritted teeth as we sweated and scraped and hauled on lines. This had become our motto.

The masts and rigging were shipped first; the hull would follow a week later. While waiting for the boat to arrive from its cross-country truck journey, we camped at the Maryland boatyard's picnic area—working in the rain and cooking meals on a one-burner gas stove that was set up in an open-air rigging shed. As the proper yachtsmen were applying finishing touches to Hinckleys, Sabres, and Grand Banks yachts, coming and going from their gleaming vehicles, we were trying hard not to feel like mongrels as we tucked into plates of indescribable hash or attempted to clean up by wiping our filthy brows with a rag.

Using paint scrapers, we stripped the masts bare and restored a bright finish with a drippy mixture of Vaseline and raw linseed oil. We had all developed blisters and an acute pain between our shoulders from the scraping motion. When it wasn't pouring rain, the late-spring sun burned our pale New England skin. When the hull arrived, we stepped the masts and quickly rigged the shrouds, bent on the five sails, and reeved the miles of lines. I was reminded of Ernest Shackleton who, when camped on Elephant Island after crossing the Drake Passage from Antarctica, his men frostbitten and wrapped in rotting sealskin sleeping bags, had quipped, "I hope you're all enjoying my little party."

My friends—at least, they were my friends when we started this little adventure—were reaching their limits and were growing testy. Thankfully, we launched *Bagheera*, and the engine purred like a cat as we fired it off. We hastily tuned the rig, tossed the

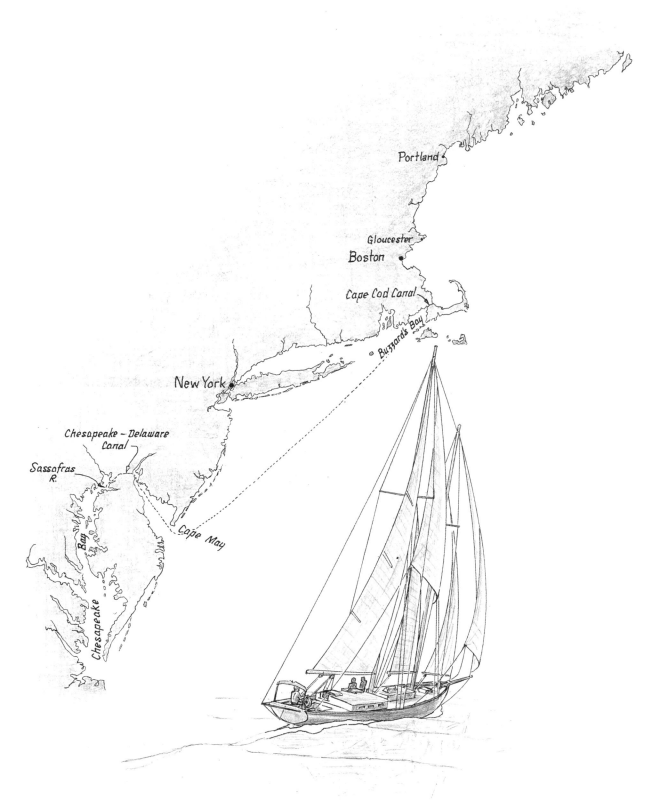

The journey from Maryland's Eastern Shore was smooth and, once offshore of New Jersey, the old schooner began to stomp down the rhumb line towards Buzzards Bay.

remaining gear aboard, and headed north. Our course would take us out of the Sassa-fras River, north through the Chesapeake and into the Chesapeake-Delaware Canal, out Delaware Bay, and to sea around Cape May. We would sail outside Long Island. It would take us the better part of two days and two nights to reach New England.

Once through the Cape Cod Canal we would draw a bead on the seabuoy off Port-land and stomp down the rhumb line, the sheets wung-out on a reach that would make the old schooner plow along like a train down a hill. We would drop our sails briefly for a shot through the Canal, and then off we'd go.

The voyage proved to be as smooth as we'd imagined for the first two days. We enjoyed balmy, early-spring weather through the Chesapeake and down Delaware Bay—sailing around Cape May and offshore without incident. Our luck held through the night as we kept outside of Long Island's Montauk Point and across the Long Island Sound. Instead, our luck suddenly changed as we entered Buzzard's Bay, Mass., and began to drop sail to prepare for our entrance into the Cape Cod Canal.

When we engaged the engine into what was supposed to be dead slow ahead, noth-ing happened. That is to say the rpm increased, but we continued to sit stock-still in the water, the stone monument marking the Canal entrance off our port quarter remaining in the same relative position.

Huh? I took the engine out of gear and tried again. There was no accompanying *thunk*, only the smooth sound of the engine revving without a load. We had either lost the linkage in the transmission or . . . our propeller. I peered over the side, a crewmem-ber holding tight to my ankles. Sure enough, the aperture appeared as a big hole through which I could clearly see, unencumbered by the dark shape of the propeller, the green water on the other side of the boat shining in the morning sun.

We were a few hundred yards from the entrance to the Canal, the southerly wind blowing right up the slot so that we were running out of sea room, and we had no pro-peller. I was briefly tempted to try sailing through—I was desperate, and the already anxious crew had smelled the barn—but I read in the Canal guide that it was strictly forbidden, and that any vessel caught doing so would be admonished via radio, possibly fined, and towed to shore. What to do?

I explained to the crew—there were seven of us—that we would have to set sail quickly and tack back out of Buzzard's Bay to gain sea room until we came up with a plan to get to Maine. Maybe we could haul out at New Bedford, Mass., and find a propeller. But it was Friday morning of Memorial Day Weekend. We made a few calls, but no one would take our case. We pictured sailing right around the Cape and dismissed the idea because of the distance. But the prospect of sitting on a mooring in New Bedford for three or four days, or a week, as we hunted down a propeller and waited our turn to be hauled out of the water appealed to no one.

Maybe we could get a tow through the Canal and sail the rest of the way, somebody, I can't remember who, suggested. With this in mind, we listened to the marine forecast again and wrote down what was predicted for the following night. West winds would build to twenty knots and clock around to the northwest around midnight, and then it would go north and finally northeast, in the early morning hours. I looked at the chart and counted off the miles—about 120 from the Canal exit to the Portland seabuoy. Even if we got a tow, I soon learned it would be several hours before they could arrive, which meant we would have to wait until the next tide cycle. This meant we wouldn't get through until after 1500. But there was plenty of wind predicted, and if we racked up the miles on a port tack, working our way parallel with the coast, maybe by the time it came northeast, pushing us offshore, we could flop over on a starboard tack and beat the rest of the way into Portland. The plan seemed pretty simple, one long reach that would become a beat only at the very end. When we were pushed too far offshore by the shifting wind, it would be time to tack anyway as we drew abeam of the seabuoy.

We discussed our options, each person having his chance to make suggestions or voice concerns. "Does anyone want to get off?" I asked. Anyone who didn't want to keep going under these circumstances could get off with the tug and catch a bus home.

We had talked ourselves into it. As long as we kept a plan in our back pockets and a harbor to duck into (Provincetown, Gloucester, Portsmouth), we would be in good shape. We might drift, but it didn't sound likely. We were a sailboat. We should sail.

The "tug" was a Towboat/US vessel sporting a pair of 300-hp outboards on its transom. We rounded up off Hog Island at 1330 and passed the towline's bridle through our hawsepipes. We felt silly—a flaccid crew of a once-proud schooner being towed on the end of a wire by what looked like a Boston Whaler—as we hung around on deck, watching the joggers and cyclists move along the Canal's footpath on this otherwise perfect spring day. Every now and then someone would wave at us, an old man sitting on a bench, a Red Sox cap on his head and a pair of large earphones clapped to his ears, or a young mother pushing a jogging stroller. We occasionally chatted with the tug skipper over the radio, but there was little to do except steer.

It was 1515 by the time we dropped the tow. We immediately raised the main, mainstaysail, forestaysail, and jib and fell off on a reach that was soon pushing us along at eight knots. The wind was westerly, blowing over the land, so there was no sea running as we plowed along, our spirits restored. Provincetown dropped out of sight under our starboard quarter, and just before dark I called all hands to put a reef in the main. The wind had built to about eighteen knots, and I knew I would thank myself for this later if the wind continued to build. I had split the watch with the mate, tugboat style, so that he was standing the 1800 to midnight watch. I ducked below for some rest after the crew toasted the boat—a splash even tossed in the bilge—with a slug of Gosling's rum.

When I came on deck at midnight, the wind had shifted northwesterly and was blowing at considerably more than twenty knots. An hour later it was blowing straight out of the north, a little earlier than had been forecast, and was gusting to more than thirty knots. We had taken in the jib, still making good time under the reefed main and two staysails, but we were losing ground too early, and the seas were beginning to build until they were steep and breaking and washing green water down the deck.

The three of us on watch were clipped into the jackline, which had been rigged in a triangle shape from the quarter bitts forward to the mainmast. We could remain clipped in as we dropped into the main companionway to do a boat check or plot our position. (We were navigating by GPS and DR, having also taken sun sights on the leg from Cape May to Buzzard's Bay.)

By 0400 the boat was laboring in the steep waves, and we were being pushed farther offshore. The wind had shifted to the north and stayed there, blowing steady thirty knots and gusting well over forty. We dropped the main and tacked, and I realized that unless the wind shifted northeast soon, we would make no progress toward Portland.

Suddenly I felt the creep of fear begin tugging at the pit of my stomach. It happened in an instant. One moment we were bashing along in the seas and it was a great adventure, and the next the picture took on a serious pallor—one involving a boat overwhelmed by the heavy seas and unremitting wind. Then came the shame, the sense of dread invoked by the realization that I brought the situation on myself, put these other young men at risk through a series of well-intentioned but slightly cavalier decisions. The prudent choice would have been to pull into New Bedford and have the boat hauled out and refitted with a new propeller whenever the yard's schedule allowed. Sailing is like that; incidents occur and no one's schedule matters a whit. It's when you force a schedule when prudence dictates otherwise that trouble begins to brew. And such is the nature of a storm at sea: you bark your shins on everything, you enjoy very little sleep, you eat bad food, you're wet through, and you promise yourself you'll never do it again, if only you could be safely ushered home by an unseen, benevolent force.

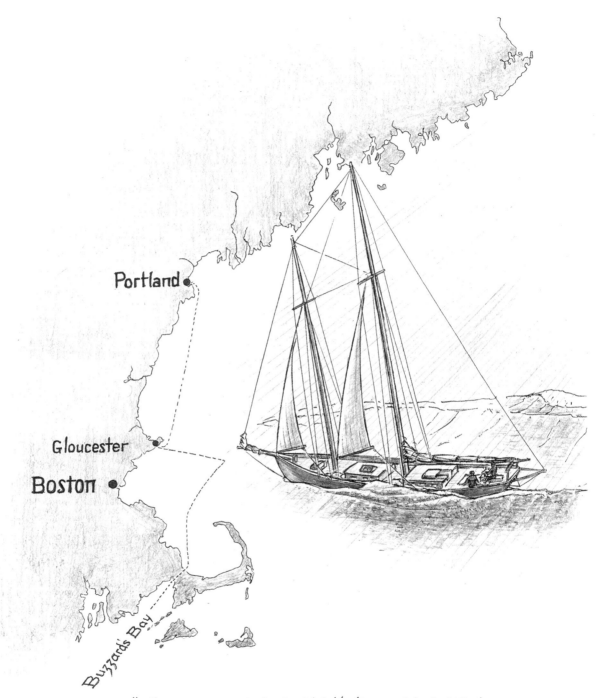

"When I came on deck at midnight, the wind had shifted northwesterly and was blowing considerably more than 20 knots."

The boat was creaking and groaning, and the rigging, I realized, had not been tuned as carefully as I would have liked. For some reason the hyperbole of Rockwell Kent came to mind. He always had a way of shouting out at the overwhelming force of nature, in this case while he was crashing along in a storm in the Cabot Strait: "The darkness and the wind! The imponderable immensity of space and elements! My frail hands grip the tiller; my eyes stare hypnotically at the stars beyond the tossing masthead or watch the boat wave as we part the seas. I hold the course."

A more apt literary reference, although it didn't come to mind that night, might well be Longfellow's *Wreck of the Hesperus*. In the poem, the prideful captain ignores warnings of foul weather and proceeds to sail headlong into a cruel storm—off Gloucester, Massachusetts, no less.

"Last night the moon had a golden ring,
And to-night no moon we see!"
The skipper he blew a whiff from his pipe,
And a scornful laugh laughed he.
Colder and louder blew the wind,
A gale from the north-east;
The snow fell hissing in the brine,
And the billows frothed like yeast.

At some point on that cold, miserable night, I made the choice to turn back for Gloucester. Twenty to twenty-five knots and a few breaking waves was one thing. Thirty to forty knots and green water washing down the decks of an old boat that deserved better—plus a seasick crew—was no one's idea of a good time. We turned back at 0500, taking the wind and waves on our starboard quarter, and immediately the motion eased. I remembered with some disgust the old refrain, "Gentlemen don't go to weather." The dawn broke clear as I lay below for a nap.

We would need another tow in from the seabuoy off Gloucester, which we arranged easily enough. When we got to the dock at Roe's Marine we learned that the yard crew had generously offered to stay an extra hour to help us, and before long *Bagheera* was in slings and lifted free of the water. The propeller shaft looked naked and a little ridiculous without its propeller; there was no visible damage. The nuts must have vibrated themselves loose on the 3,000-mile journey overland, not loose enough to notice with a quick check from a wrench—but imperceptibly loose enough to fall off after a few days at sea.

We fitted the new prop into place and, miraculously, we were underway again by 1600, steaming northward under diesel power.

Instead of the hero's welcome we had imagined, we were greeted by darkness and silence as we limped ignominiously into Portland Harbor at 0230 Sunday morning, my security call on Channel 16 ringing hollowly over the airwaves—feeling every bit

Longfellow's "Wreck of the Hesperus." (In fact, having sailed past Norman's Woe near Gloucester, we had narrowly missed the same fate.)

We docked at Peaks Island's public landing, our sails bunched in clumps on their spars, our jerry jugs lashed crookedly to the rails, our sunken eyes and unshaven faces reminiscent of the haunted Ancient Mariner—or the zombies from *Night of the Living Dead*. But, we told each other as we walked home through the quiet streets, *Bagheera* was finally home in Maine.

I have done numerous deliveries over the years; most were without incident, but some, like the one detailed above, are fraught with challenges that simply can't be predicted. But in the *Bagheera* adventure I ignored the most salient tool in my weather-prediction toolchest: sound judgment. The post-mortem lessons of that trip are clear enough now. The boat was old but it was new to me. I had sailed it only once before and not on my home waters but in San Francisco Bay. I had to reassemble the boat and rig from total chaos—literally, piles of rigging stacked on pallets—in a mad rush. I still recall the four-page fax that the former owner sent to me at the yard, which was a handwritten diagram of how to reassemble the rig. Which blocks to put where, which shackles and pins to go in which piece of deck hardware. And most of the rigging had lost their accompanying tags on the cross-country journey, so reassembly was like a nightmarish SAT problem involving process of elimination. We did not wait for the right weather; nor did we have the luxury of doing so. Each of my friends had tight schedules, jobs, and families to return to. It turned out all right, but I still shudder to think of what could have happened.

The following items are of invaluable interest to the sailor when contemplating weather at sea. I provide a brief description of how to use them intelligently, but whole books are written on each subject for further clarification. I merely offer them as a bare minimum of tools to employ.

INTERNET SOURCES

The Internet is probably the single, most-valuable tool for anyone planning a sailing trip, whether for a day or a week. The National Weather Service publishes free myriad sources of weather information, culled from numerous on-site weather buoys, satellite and radar data, and even airplanes. You can select the analysis by meteorologists or examine the real-time data yourself. This is all available online at no cost and is one of the true benefits of American tax dollars. The web site weather.gov (and not the commercial site weather.com, which is choked with advertising and is generally geared toward enjoying the out-of-doors for golfing) is a trove of information on real-time weather data and predictions. There are too many commercial and nonprofit web sites to describe here. And their options change daily. But for solid reliability and a broad array of information, the National Weather Service is one place to start.

MARINE RADIO

Every marine radio is equipped with a weather channel. Usually marked "WX," the button allows you to tune into the National Weather Service's local broadcast for the waters in your area. Until relatively recently, this was a live person reading the broadcast into the microphone. Some years ago I visited the NWS office in Gray, Maine, and met the handful of men (they were all men) whose voices I had been listening to for years. It was like visiting Hollywood for Maine sailors. Unfortunately, those days are gone, and the human voices are replaced by the ubiquitous "Iron Mike," that computer-generated voice that mangles certain words, especially place names with unusual pronunciations.

But the forecast is just as good as ever because it's still analyzed by these same human beings. It's just that it's far cheaper to program a computer than to pay someone to read the forecast for hours on end.

I make a habit of listening to the forecast every morning prior to heading out on a sailing trip of even a few hours' duration. I sit down with a notebook and take notes on wind direction and velocity, its predicted change over the course of the day, and what's in store for the following day. The forecast is always preceded by a big-picture overview that mentions the systems themselves, the highs and lows, and how they're interacting with one another in the region. It's incredibly helpful, especially when you listen every day, since it begins to make sense and you begin to appreciate the patterns that emerge and repeat themselves. In Maine, for example, every sailor knows that the northwest wind is a clearing wind. The sky will be silvery and bright, the wind fresh and steady, clear and dry, as it blows over the land. This will also mean that there won't be much of a sea running close to shore, since the wind has limited fetch.

By taking notes I am not really listening to the immediate forecast, just jotting everything down as quickly as possible. Then, after the computer voice blathers on for a few minutes about temperatures elsewhere in the region and "heating-degree days" and what the highest and lowest recorded temperatures are on this particular day in history, the marine forecast is repeated, first the Coastal Waters (out to twenty-five nautical miles) and then followed by the Offshore Waters. I correct my notes or add to them, and then I shut off the radio. Here in my hands, these few scratches in shorthand ("NNW 10-15 kts → 15-20 kts in aft.," for example), is all I need to know about what kind of day it will be. The wind direction tells me which destinations are feasible, based on which anchorages will offer shelter and which will be exposed to the wind and waves. The predicted velocity tells me how far I can expect to get, whether I need to put a reef in the mainsail, and how wet we will get if we have to make long tacks on a close reach. (You get wetter going into the wind and waves.)

BAROMETER

It seems funny to advocate use of the barometer in these times of ubiquitous electronics. In this age of the Internet, can a simple analog barometer still be considered necessary? Is it even relevant? That relic of the 19th century, that piece of brass and glass that you see old-timers tapping and squinting at in classic movies or in scenes from Joseph Conrad stories. Gearheads will snort; computer nerds will guffaw. But, yes! A barometer is both relevant and necessary, and, if you take the time to learn how to use one—it isn't hard—you will grow to look upon it as a dear friend. Simply put, a barometer measures atmospheric pressure on the surface of the earth. And by noting its pressure over time, hourly, for example, you begin to build a pattern in your logbook of how the *actual* weather, not the *predicted* weather, is taking shape. A steady barometer means steady weather. One that rises or falls quickly (over a period of a few hours) means harsh conditions are brewing.

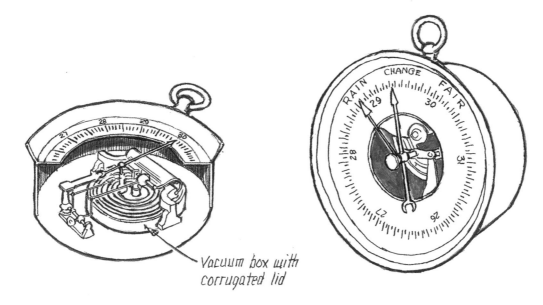

Vacuum box with
corrugated lid

The analog, aneroid barometer operates
with average-pressure air sealed
within a cylindrical metal box. Change
of air pressure outside the box due
to "highs" and "lows" of passing weather
systems cause the lid to press inward
or outward — mechanically activating
the pointer leading to the dial.

One of the best, and simplest, books on weather is by Americana expert Eric Sloane. *Weather Book*, published in 1949, is slim, only ninety pages, but its simple black-and-white illustrations with handwritten callouts (like the book in your hands) make it instructive and a joy to read. Sloane's section on the barometer offers a few jewels; the first is this notion of barometric change.

"Here is something important to remember: the actual reading on a barometer is often very little indication of anything," he writes. "The thing one really wants to know is if the barometer is rising, steady, or unsteady. In this way one can tell whether the present outside weather is liable to change and, if so, whether for better or worse." By way of example, Sloane also includes a table that considers prevailing winds on the coast of Massachusetts and how the attendant barometric pressure suggests the type of weather ahead. That's the frustrating thing about a weather book; you are soon drawn into local patterns that are useless to someone who lives and sails elsewhere. However, the boon of modern times—the Internet—offers so much in the way of local weather phenomena, by the Government, by aficionados, by research institutes and universities, that this information is readily available wherever you intend to sail.

RULES FOR FORETELLING THE WEATHER

(Adapted for use with aneroid barometers; contributed by
U. S. Weather Bureau.)

Barometer	Wind from	Weather indicated
High and steady	SW to NW	Fair and little temperature change for one or two days.
High and rising rapidly	SW to NW	Fair followed by warmer and rain within two days.
Very high, falling slowly	SW to NW	Fair and slowly rising temperature for two days.
High and falling slowly	S to SE	Rain within 24 hours.
High and falling rapidly	S to SE	Increasing wind with rain in 12 to 24 hours.
High and falling slowly	SE to NE	Rain in 12 to 18 hours.
High and falling rapidly	SE to NE	Increasing wind with rain in 12 hours.
High and falling slowly	E to NE	Summer—light winds, fair. Winter—rain in 24 hours.
High and falling rapidly	E to NE	Summer—rain in 12 to 24 hours. Winter—rain or snow and increasing winds.
Low and falling slowly	SE to NE	Rain will continue one or two days.
Low and falling rapidly	SE to NE	Rain and high wind; clearing and cooler in 36 hours.
Low and rising slowly	S to SW	Clearing soon and fair several days.
Low and falling rapidly	S to E	Severe storm soon, clearing and cooler in 24 hours.
Low and falling rapidly	E to N	Northeast gales with heavy rain or snow, followed in winter by cold wave.
Low and rising rapidly	Going to W	Clearing and colder.

In a short how-to article in the magazine *Ocean Navigator*, William Cook, a nautical instruments collector, provided the following short steps in acquiring and setting up a barometer for use:

1. Mount the instrument where it will remain undisturbed.
2. Determine the exact barometric pressure from a trusted Internet site or weather station.
3. Turn the adjusting screw on the back of the barometer until the indicator hand points to a reading on the dial that corresponds to your known local barometric pressure.
4. Place the reference needle over the pressure indicator hand to set the new reference mark. This will allow you to observe the direction and distance the pressure indicator hand has moved at your next reading.

Reefing —

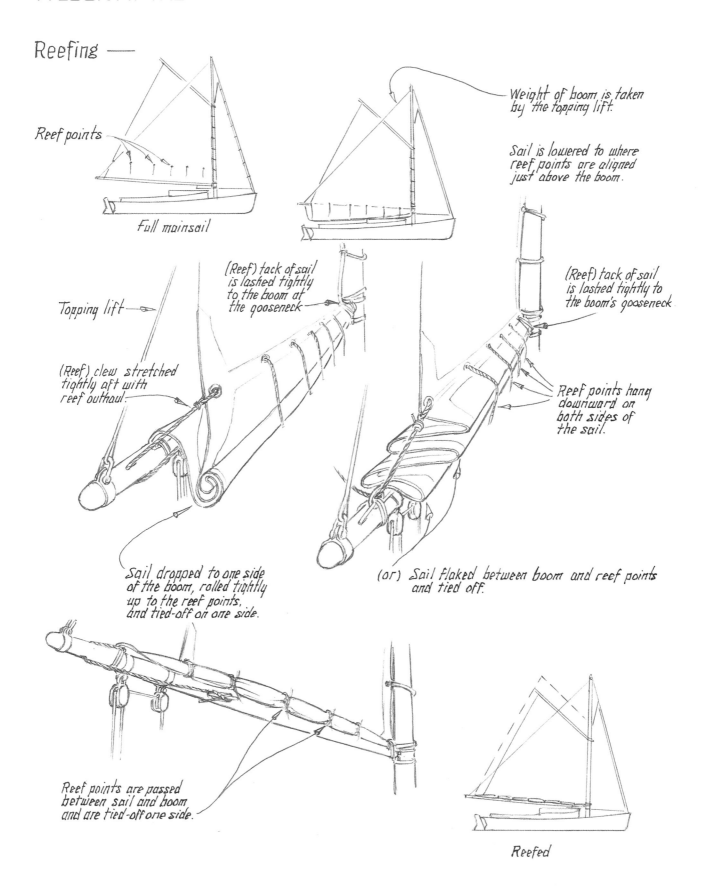

Reef points

Full mainsail

Weight of boom is taken by the topping lift.

Sail is lowered to where reef points are aligned just above the boom.

Topping lift

(Reef) tack of sail is lashed tightly to the boom at the gooseneck.

(Reef) clew stretched tightly aft with reef outhaul.

(Reef) tack of sail is lashed tightly to the boom's gooseneck.

Reef points hang downward on both sides of the sail.

Sail dropped to one side of the boom, rolled tightly up to the reef points, and tied-off on one side.

(or) Sail flaked between boom and reef points and tied off.

Reef points are passed between sail and boom and are tied-off one side.

Reefed

5. Keep in mind that the rate of change is important, as the amount of change in forecasting corresponds to changes in the weather. Checking the pressure hourly, especially during unstable weather—as part of a routine boat check—is a good idea.

6. The hands of a barometer are very light and may be affected by friction. It is advisable, therefore, to tap the barometer lightly before taking the reading. In some cases the indicator may move several points. That is normal. Simply take your reading and adjust the reference indicator to the new position.

7. Finally, keep in mind that a barometer does nothing more than measure atmospheric pressure. With this information in mind, one can make some intelligent guesses about the weather that is soon to be at hand.

A barometer may be old-fashioned, and it is certainly quaint-looking, but having one aboard (and taking the time to note its changes) is a worthwhile investment for any boat. Ken McKinley, the Maine-based meteorologist, summed up his recommendations about a shipboard barometer (in a June 2011 *Ocean Navigator* article) thus: "If only one [weather] instrument can be chosen, my suggestion is a good quality bulkhead mounted aneroid barometer. A barometer gives data that cannot be estimated without an instrument, that provides important information about where the boat is located within the larger weather pattern, and that helps predict short term weather changes."

We discussed the Beaufort Scale in the last chapter. It's worth mentioning again in the context of a discussion on weather, though, since weather is all about context. You can stand on a dock or a beach and judge how strongly the wind is blowing using the Beaufort Scale's numerical categories. This is handy when listening to or reviewing the weather report on the VHF radio or the Internet. If you see in the morning that the wind is a mere zephyr (Force 1, "Light Air"), causing a few riffles on the surface of the water, but you hear there's a small-craft advisory (Force 6, "Strong Breeze," winds greater than twenty-five knots) in effect for the afternoon, you can witness its stages of advancement as the morning progresses. But you might decide to take certain precautions, such as not inviting your skittish Aunt Hilda to sail that day or, at the very least, put a preemptive reef in the mainsail.

REEFING

Reefing means to reduce the size of the sail by rolling up and tying it in a tight roll such that the sail is smaller and therefore not as much force is exerted on the rig by the wind.

Not only are you reducing the overall sail area, you're doing so from the top down, lowering the sails' center of effort. *Swallow* has a single reef in the main. The jib is drawn without a reef, although many sloops have reef points in both the main and jib. If we were to reef *Swallow* on this particular morning, we would follow these procedures, while still at the dock or mooring:

– Raise the mainsail, using the throat and peak halyards, so that the sail is up only as far as the reef points;
– You now have a new "clew" and "tack" of the reduced-size sail;
– Lash the tack tightly to the gooseneck of the boom using spare line. You want the boom to still move independently of the mast, but you also want the tack to be drawn both tightly downward against the boom, but also secured against the leading edge in preparation for the next step;
– Tighten the "reef outhaul," the line that extends from the grommet on what will become the clew of the sail once it's reefed, until it is almost bar tight; this acts as a counterpoint to the lashings you've just secured on the new tack of the reefed sail;
– Lash the clew with spare line securely to the boom using chafe gear (spare canvas, for example) wherever the line might chafe against the sailcloth; the reef outhaul pulls the foot of the sail aft, while the lashings keep them securely snugged downward;
– Only then—after you've secured the tack and clew—should you tie the reef points themselves. Do this by tying "reef knots" (duh), but be sure to only tie the sail itself. *Do not tie the reef points around the boom.* By keeping a space between the foot of the sail and the boom, you preserve that essential foil shape the sail needs to provide lift. Otherwise, the sail becomes too flat (inefficient) and can also tear when the strain of the reef points is too severe;
– Once the foot is tied, you can then raise the sail to its full (reefed) height in the usual way. The reefed sail should be wrinkle free and look like a smaller version of its usual self, nicely shaped with a modest belly (technically, this is called "roach") and taut but not flat.

While the boat will be a little sluggish when the winds are still calm while sailing under reduced canvas, you'll thank yourself many times when the wind freshens later in the afternoon. To reef a sail in a fresh breeze is tricky indeed. Which is why it's best to follow prudence with regard to reefing; if you think you *might* need a reef, don't hesitate and put one in. On the other hand, it's exceedingly simple to shake out a reef when you're underway when you realize that the wind has not built quite as strongly as predicted and you don't actually need the reef.

To shake out a reef, simply bring the main sheet in tight and turn a little closer to the wind so that the full force of the wind is not on the sails. Then untie all the reef points, release the lashings on the clew and tack, release the reef outhaul from its cleat, and then raise the sail back up. On *Swallow* this would take about two minutes. Be sure, however, that you've removed all the reef points before raising the sail back to its full height. If one reef point is missed and you haul the sail back up in a hurry, you risk tearing the sail at the reef point because of the great strain concentrated on this one point.

TIDES AND CURRENTS

Tides move up and down; currents move horizontally. This can be confusing when discussing tidal currents, since the terms are often used interchangeably. For example, if you're sailing along and you see a current pattern in the water ahead, you might say, "It's the ebb tide." This is a slight misnomer. It's actually the ebb tidal *current* you see. But the result of this current will ultimately be low tide. (And the flood tidal current brings high tide.) Tidal current brings the tide up or down, but when referring to the movement of the tide itself, this is a vertical motion.

Another handy tool to have aboard your boat, and perhaps stuck to the refrigerator door, is a tide chart. Each tidal cycle (between high and low tide) is about six and a quarter hours apart. The tidal day is slightly longer than a solar day, about twenty-five hours, which means high and low tides occur a little later than the previous day. This is because the moon, which largely drives the tidal cycle, is rotating in the same direction that the earth spins and takes slightly longer to rotate the earth than the earth takes to rotate once on its axis. (Consider the minute hand on a clock: it passes the hour hand at 12:00 but an hour later passes the hour hand not at the "12" position but at the "1," or at 1:05—since both hands are moving in the same direction.) The gravitational pull of the sun contributes to the range of the tide, but it is more of a contributing influence than a driving factor.

The strongest tides—those with greater difference between high and low water—are caused by the combined forces of the moon and the sun. When these two bodies are aligned in their forces, during the new and full moon, the tidal change is greatest. This is called the spring tide (and has nothing to do with the season of the same name).

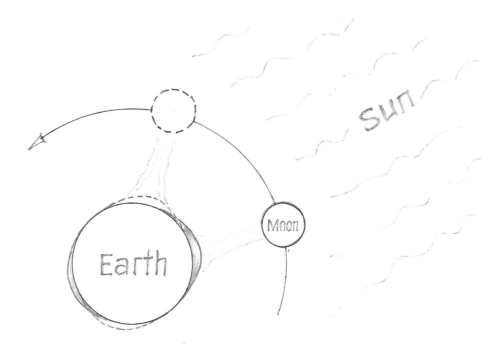

The ocean tide is the hump of water raised under the moon by force of moon's gravity as it circles our globe in a 25+hour daily circuit. Directly opposite in the Earth's oceans is a similar high tide hump also lifted by gravitational pull and by centrifugal force as it progresses westward. Between the two humps are the low tide areas where the encircling seas are stretched thin.

Beyond the moon is the sun — magnifying the moon's pull when moon and sun are aligned, causing **spring tides**. Or minimizing the pull — causing **neap tides** — when moon and sun are at right angles to the earth.

When these forces are working against one another, on the first and third quarter of the lunar cycle, these forces are pulling against one another and therefore causing lesser tidal range. This is called a neap tide.

Unfortunately, the tides are not only affected by the moon and sun but also to a great degree by water depth and local topography. "The relatively simpler problem of tides on an ocean of uniform depth covering the entire earth was worked out by Laplace (1774), but with little resemblance to observed conditions," wrote William van Torn in his epic tome *Oceanography and Seamanship*. "Since then, the history of tidal theory includes many attempts to apply the equations of Laplace to the real oceans, introducing actual sea-floor topography, observed density stratification (which profoundly alters the

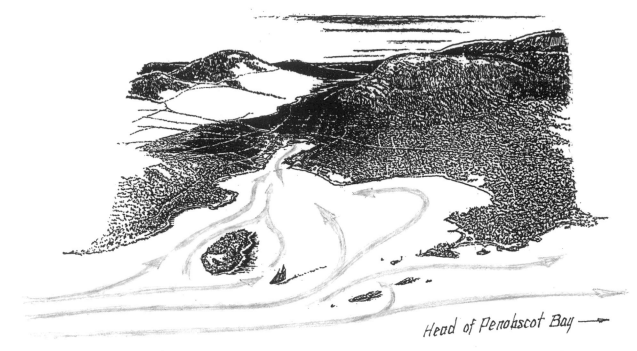

Head of Penobscot Bay ⟶

⟵ Gulf of Maine and open sea

Pattern of tidal current entering Maine's Camden Harbor during period of maximum flood, twice daily, with velocity to 1½ knots. Incoming tidal current is slowed by freshwater river current exiting the inner harbor.

character of flow in certain areas), frictional dissipation, and our old friend the Coriolis force. Even with these concessions to realism, however, the tidal equations cannot be solved mathematically."

In other words, get a tide chart. It will show the daily tides for a broad array of local towns, effectively covering an entire region.

It's important to know that charts give depths at what is called "Mean Lower Low Water." This means that the soundings given on charts are the mean of the lowest of the low tides. Which does not mean that the depth at a particular spot is often at the exact depth it says it is, simply that it's roughly what it says it is—*at low tide*. It can be shallower, in the event of an unusually low low tide (during a powerful spring tide, for example); or it can be deeper (during a modest neap tide, for example). So you should not take charted depths as gospel! Rather, they are an approximation of what you can expect for depth in a given area.

A more confused pattern of tidal current enhanced by river current departing Camden Harbor at maximum ebb — as experienced by rowers and sailers of small boats.

An extreme example of a tidal current is a tidal bore. A bore is a tidal current, but it is particularly powerful as a result of local geographic conditions. For example, on the Amazon River during certain spring tides, you can expect a wall of water twenty-five feet high to rush upriver at a rate of twelve to fourteen knots! More common tidal bores, on the Maine Coast or amongst the islands of the Pacific Northwest and Alaska, are more modest. But they can be strong nonetheless and certainly worthy of our respect from our position aboard the deck of a small boat such as *Swallow*.

In summary, the vicissitudes of wind and wave will conspire against you. Yet using certain basic tools in a regular way so that you become proficient with them will empower you to understand the context of each of them and, therefore, how local weather conditions will affect your day.

5

CHARTS & NAVIGATION

"'A very fine landfall, Mr. Marshall,' said Jack, coming down from the top, where he had been scrutinizing the cape through his glass. 'The Astronomer Royal could not have done better.'"

—from *Master and Commander*, by Patrick O'Brian

I awoke to the sound of dripping. My sheets and blankets felt slightly damp, and there was a clammy feel to the air. The dripping was not constant, like a rain shower, but more scattered and irregular. A heavy drip here, another one a second or two later. On deck I was greeted by the thick Maine fog that has been the bane of every sailor since the earliest European fishermen had discovered cod on the Grand Banks. No doubt this same fog had vexed the Indians for eons prior. It was "dungeon thick," as they say. We could see nothing about us except the grim, gray murk, even though we were closely surrounded by moored boats only a stone's-throw away in all directions. We could hear noises from the town itself, only a tenth of a mile across the water—the chatter of fishermen on the piers, the roar of an engine going uphill, the clanking of floating wharves against the docks—but saw nothing but gray.

On this particular morning, I had to chart my course carefully, raise anchor, and navigate the schooner *Mercantile* from Stonington across Penobscot Bay to Camden—some twenty miles away to the west. I would have to do whether the fog lifted or not, since the passengers, still asleep below, would have planes to catch or other vacation commitments to keep.

I pulled the chart from its storage locker and stared at it. I knew every rock between the anchorage and the destination, having sailed these waters, indeed, this exact course, many dozens of times before. I had played in these waters as a child, zipping around in my grandfather's Boston Whaler with my family, landing on the islands of Merchant Row and exploring the coves and beaches for natural treasures and other loot. In many ways, it was my backyard, and, even if I didn't have a chart, I could likely find my way. Yet fog has a way of challenging your basest instincts. You're stripped of any way to check your position visually, requiring blind faith in your navigational skills. Like flying by instruments in an airplane in the dark. You know they don't lie, yet you have no immediate proof that they're leading you to your intended destination. I had a twisted feeling in my gut; when I held the dividers to the chart, I noticed my hands were shaking.

Placing one point of my dividers on the left-hand grid, the latitude, of the chart, I carefully set the other point at the next minute of latitude—one nautical mile. I then "walked" my way from our anchorage in Stonington westward, out the Deer Isle Thorofare, through the Fox Island Channel, and across the remaining stretch of water to Curtis Island Light that marks the entrance to Camden Harbor. I did this a few times, not because I wasn't sure of the distance or the route, but as a way to reassure myself of what was true—the location of ledges and islands, the sound signals on buoys and lighthouses along the way, the location of the nun and can buoys that were not rigged with gongs or bells but were marked with painted numbers. It was not a straight westward passage, more of an improvisation on a westerly theme, peppered with rocks the whole way. The big test was the four-mile crossing of East Penobscot Bay. Until then, I would have buoys close enough together to engage in a kind of blind-man's-bluff-connect-the-dots. But it was this one passage I was most concerned about. The wind was southerly; the tidal current northerly, meaning they were coming from the same direction. I was sure to be set northward along my course; this I knew. On a piece of scratch paper I sketched out a simple set-and-drift problem that contemplated a two-knot current and the roughly six knots of speed I expected this old schooner to make in this moderate breeze. An old lumber- and stone-hauling boat, it had not been built to sail close to the weather. It was a wide, heavy boat, twenty-two feet in the beam and about eighty feet on the waterline, and not at all sprightly. It needed a fair wind to keep it moving in a straight line, and while the large centerboard helped, it would do little to keep the boat from being set north of our entrance to the next channel.

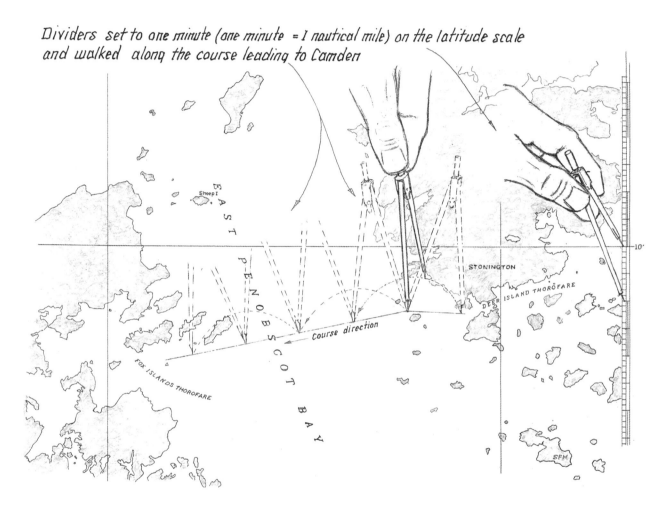

Dividers set to one minute (one minute = 1 nautical mile) on the latitude scale and walked along the course leading to Camden

For my part, set-and-drift calculations have always seemed speculative, at best, especially when sailing and navigating short-handedly, as I was then. In *How to Abandon Ship*, a tidy little book published during World War II about the barest of skills needed to survive and navigate in deprived conditions at sea, authors Phil Richards and John J. Banigan put this thought more succinctly: "If you are an untrained man, you do not concern yourself with the set of the current. Your guess as to allowance will undoubtedly be out of proportion." Whether unskilled or shorthanded, the most one can hope for in these situations is a proverbial nod in the direction of the current when one is figuring out one's course.

I descended to the galley and poured myself a cup of coffee from the Shipmate stove and returned to the deck, pacing up and down and trying to imagine, by peering intently over the rail, that the fog was lifting. By 8:00 AM the fog was just as thick, and we had to get underway if we were to make our arrival time. I called up the deckhand and mate and explained our course. One of them would be needed up in the bow to act as lookout, while the other would help manage the sails as I was left to steer and navigate alone (with the passengers chatting amiably in my ear). The schooners of the Maine coastal fleet are designed to make money for their owners, so sailing shorthanded is an accepted way of life. The Coast Guard makes minimum recommendations for crew, but none other than the captain requires training of any kind. I was essentially on my own when it came to navigating.

We hoisted anchor and, under power of the diesel yawl boat, nosed our way through the channel, following the compass since we couldn't see more than 100 feet in any direction. As the passengers finished their breakfast and emerged on deck, the mate put them to work hoisting sails. Soon we were clipping along under the "four lowers," main, foresail, staysail, and jib, and we killed the engine. The breeze was strong enough to keep us moving, and without the engine running we could be more attuned to the approaching clang of bell and gong buoys.

After reaching the end of the Thorofare, I adjusted our course consistent with my previous calculation and sailed off across the open water into the fog. I looked at my watch as the last buoy slipped into the murk behind us and noted the time in the log. Gripping the wheel had stopped the shaking in my hands, but the pain in my stomach was still there. A half hour passed. And then a few more minutes. And then a few more.

At roughly the appointed time, the lookout cried out that he saw the shape of an island ahead; the jagged, black shapes of spruces emerged in a ghostly hue just 100 feet off the bow. I steadied the course to pass the island to starboard, but as we drew close, I realized, with absolute horror, that this was not the island I had expected. It was far too small. In fact, I had no idea which island it was. With the shape distorted by fog, and no other islands visible, I frantically searched the chart for some clue as to what it was. Rocks are everywhere on the Maine coast. It is only your constant navigational awareness that keeps you from hitting them. And here I was without a clue as to what island I was looking at. The only thing I knew with certainty was that I had crossed East

Penobscot Bay and had arrived at one of the many dozens of islands that form the cluster called the Fox Islands, spanning some five miles, north to south. Either I had overcompensated for the set of the current or undercompensated—each could be true, since there were spruce-covered islands just to the north of the channel entrance and just as many to the south. I was lost in the fog with a complement of twenty-eight passengers.

Now, this was in the early days of GPS when the units were several hundred dollars apiece. The owner of this boat, however, had not purchased one; nor had he purchased a radar set. He had equipped the boat with an ancient box compass, a device that was probably original to the schooner and probably had not been swung (calibrated) since its construction some eighty years before. I had every reason to believe, therefore, that there was considerable error in the compass. Every boat has ferrous metal on it, which means each boat will have its own "deviation," the error introduced by the vessel itself—from the steel in the rig or its fastenings and hardware. This is why most commercial vessels, indeed, most vessels of any size, have compasses professionally swung to produce a small deviation card that is mounted next to the compass. There was no such card.

The local "variation," the degree to which magnetic north differs from true north, was simple enough to factor out of my navigation: it is printed on every chart on the inside of each printed compass rose. By factoring out the local variation, you can plot in true direction so that the view you have of the chart correlates with the geographical features around you.

I decided to concentrate my efforts on this island. If I studied the coast carefully enough, I hoped, I could determine some telltale clue as to its identity. It wasn't large, so we had soon circumnavigated it. The only problem was the constant haranguing by the passengers. I had to steer this large old schooner with one hand, deflect probing questions from a half-dozen chipper vacationers, keep an eye on the shore close aboard, and all the while—hoping to hell that we didn't drive into a submerged ledge—frantically study the shapes of islands on the chart and compare them to what I saw in front of me.

The mystery was solved soon enough. This was Sheep Island—the bald top gave it away—and I was soon gliding through the protected waters of the Fox Island Thorofare. The rest of the journey was more connect-the-dots with buoys. But the morning's adventure had taught me a valuable lesson that is an imperative in the darkness or fog: you simply must have a back-up plan when Plan A fails. I had allowed the pressure of time and schedule to get the better of me. With the inadequate compass, lack of radar, and short-handed crew, I should have proceeded more cautiously, taken a longer, better-marked route that would have had numerous safety nets should one intended target be missed. In the end, the only damage was to my nerves.

The practice of navigation has not always been free to an inquisitive mind. More than 300 years ago, the skill was considered proprietary and knowledge of its practices by a person not privileged to have such skill, at least in the Royal Navy, was a crime punishable by death. The Scilly Naval disaster of 1707 (described in a wonderful chapter in Dava Sobel's masterpiece *Longitude*) involved a fleet of English naval ships sailing from Gibraltar home for England. The vessels, there were twenty-nine in all, were sailing in convoy and navigating by "dead reckoning"—the logging of a vessel's course and speed through the water. The vessels had been beset by storms for several days, making decent sights of the sun difficult, which meant that the fleet's navigators could not precisely determine the vessels' exact position. That is to say, there was some doubt as to the vessels' actual positions at sea. But one seaman suspected that the position of the fleet was some distance north of where the official position, those logged and announced by the vessels' quartermasters, was considered to be. This presented a dilemma for the young navigator: should he report his suspicions and perhaps save the fleet from being wrecked on the rocks that dot the approaches to England's southwest harbors or should he report his fears and risk being court martialed? The story goes that the unofficial navigator chose to heed his conscience and report his fears. He was immediately hanged, and shortly thereafter four ships were wrecked with a loss of more than 1,400 lives.

Not until after the American Revolution would navigation be promulgated freely. This was the result of the work of a young mathematician named Nathaniel Bowditch who published a book that broke open the secret world of navigation. *The American Practical Navigator* was published in 1805, and the ancient navigational barrier was forever broken. Suddenly, any seaman who was literate and competent at his sums could learn to navigate. The book, affectionately known by pundits simply as *Bowditch*, has been continuously published by the US Government ever since.

Now, *Bowditch* is not a book to be trifled with by the aspiring coastal sailor. It is truly a navigational tome, as its subtitle, *An Epitome of Navigation and Nautical Astronomy*, suggests. It includes vast tables on the world's tidal data and ice movements, withering detail and formulae on the geometry of the Sumner Line and performing Lunar Distances (at least, until very recently), and even a comprehensive chapter on the techniques of marine surveying."

But it opens simply enough with a definition of the word navigation: "That science, generally termed *Navigation*, which affords the knowledge necessary to conduct a ship from point to point upon the earth, enabling the mariner to determine, with a sufficient degree of accuracy, the position of his vessel at any time, is properly divided into two branches: *Navigation* and *Nautical Astronomy*." Even today, *Bowditch* is a graduate-level text and really only worth exploring once the basics of navigation are understood.

For our purposes here we'll focus only on the one word—navigation—and supply enough details (not nearly so many as *Bowditch*) to afford a modest knowledge of *coastal* navigation.

The only tools you need to be a competent coastal navigator are a watch, a chart, an accurate, oil-filled compass, a pair of dividers, and a set of parallel rules. The rest, as they say, is details. You don't even need to know what these tools are at this point, but it helps to know that mastering these few simple tools is really all there is to it. Aboard *Swallow* we would have the compass mounted on a bulkhead or, best of all, on a free-standing binnacle in the center of the cockpit. This allows you to move around the compass a full 360 degrees, positioning the compass between you and any object you would like to get a "bearing" on: a point of land, another boat, a buoy, or the direction of the wind. This is more difficult to do with a compass mounted against a bulkhead, of course, but it's not impossible, especially if the compass is mounted such that you can see the whole dial instead of only half of it at any given time. And the other tools, except the wristwatch, would be packed in a sealable container, such as a Tupperware box, and kept inside a locker in the cockpit. These tools are a navigator's best friend.

Lastly, the navigator's toolbox is useless without a chart. The navigational methods I describe here make use of a paper chart. This is not to say that electronic charts don't have their place. Most commercial ships today navigate without paper for their hourly position fixes. The ubiquity of electronics is a fine development; yet a lack of appreciation for the wizardry behind them is dangerous indeed. Everyone who takes a boat to sea should know how to use a paper chart.

So let's take these tools one at a time.

CHART

According to the National Geospatial-Intelligence Agency (NGA), the federal agency that disseminates charts in the United States, "A Nautical Chart is a graphic portrayal of the marine environment showing the nature and form of the coast, the general configuration of the sea bottom including water depths, locations of dangers to navigation, locations and characteristics of man-made aids to navigation, and other features useful to the mariner."

I went to a Waldorf school, which means I have an insatiable predilection for taking a given subject, in this case cartography, and finding ways to make it more colorful and interactive than the NGA's definition. Waldorf students are urged to tell and listen to stories and draw pictures of every subject, shading them in with color. In chemistry we drew the elements in their natural state; in biology we drew mitosis and miosis, carefully shading each cell with different colors; in geometry we drew pentagons and dodecahedrons, all their parts colored and shaded like the patterns of a quilt. In English and art history we illustrated the myths and legends with knights and dragons, scenes of romance and adventure. It was a picaresque education, but it can also be an obsessive habit—seeing nothing as complete unless it has been illustrated and shaded—and is a habit that, even into adulthood, we find tough to shake.

In my navigational practices, this has meant that I've always drawn on my charts, annotated arrivals and departures, and made drawings of occurrences with notes on dates and the company I was keeping. This was in part inspired by stories I'd heard of this practice by shipmasters during the Age of Exploration, who often created their own charts of their sea routes and kept them carefully guarded as trade secrets. A favorable anchorage, for example, gave them a competitive edge over other masters, as did knowledge of local wind and current patterns or lucrative fishing grounds. All this information was annotated and illustrated on charts.

I was recently at a school reunion, in which I got to talking with a former classmate about a recent trip to Bermuda, in which he served as the boat's navigator. He, too, admitted to having felt his Waldorf education surging from his fingertips during the voyage, almost unwillingly, as he plotted progress on the charts. "I shaded everything with colored pencils," he told me. "The currents in one color, the winds another; the land masses a different color. When the others in the crew saw what I had done, they said, 'Holy shit!'" A piece of navigational notation had become a kind of impromptu art exhibit.

Whether you have these inclinations or not, illustrating and annotating your home-waters charts is exceedingly helpful for your future visits to various anchorages. And it makes a fascinating illustrated history of your sailing adventures that might, someday, become worthy of hanging on your wall.

Let's start with the earth's imaginary grid system, latitude and longitude. On a Mercator-projection chart (the most common projection for navigational charts), all lines of both latitude and longitude are presented as parallel. This is a mathematical trick to make navigation easier, but you must not forget that it is not true. This fact is most important when determining distance on a chart. Latitude lines, which really *are* parallel, are what you use to measure distance on a chart. By placing dividers one minute of latitude apart—along the left- or right-hand edge of the chart—you have measured one nautical mile (6,076 feet) of distance. Compare this same span to the longitude grid along the top or bottom of a chart, and you'll see considerable discrepancy. This is because lines of longitude draw closer together the further you get from the Equator until they meet at the North and South poles. So, only at the Equator are one minute of latitude and one minute of longitude equal to one another.

Latitude is measured north and south of the Equator up to 90 degrees. The tropics, Cancer and Capricorn, are at 23½ degrees north and south latitude respectively. (This is because the earth is tilted 23½ degrees on its axis.) At the risk of delving too deeply into *Bowditch*'s nautical astronomy portion, let me simply add that the sun's position on earth—its geographic position, the point on earth over which the sun is at its zenith at any given moment—is always within the two tropical latitude lines. It moves northward in spring until, on or about June 21st (summer solstice) when it reaches the Tropic of Cancer, it then begins to move southward. It crosses the Equator on or about September 21st (autumnal equinox) until, on or about December 21st (winter solstice), it bottoms out at the Tropic of Capricorn. Then it moves northward again, crossing the Equator on or about March 21st (vernal equinox). And so on. This is crucial to understanding the beginnings of celestial navigation, but for our purposes as coastal sailors it is relevant only insofar as we want to understand the machinations of sunrise and sunset. The times will vary according to the above schedule—the days grow longer between December and June and grow shorter a few minutes each day after the summer solstice.

Longitude lines have no such celestial parameters. The sun's geographic position simply moves westward around the earth at the rate of 15 degrees of longitude per hour so that it can complete its 360-degree rotation in twenty-four hours. (The earth, therefore, is divided into twenty-four, 15-longitudinal-degree time zones.) We calculate longitude westward and eastward from the Prime Meridian (or Greenwich Meridian) until we get to 180 degrees in either direction. This imaginary line, which actually zigzags its way from the North Pole to the South Pole through the Pacific Ocean, is called the

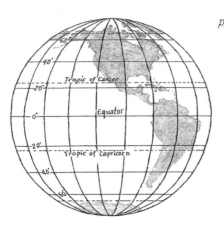

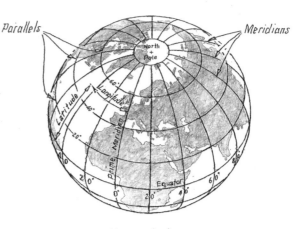

Latitude:

Distance or location **north or south** of the Equator as delineated by parallels and measured in degrees and minutes of arc.

1 minute of latitude = 1 nautical mile.

Longitude:

Distance or location **east or west** of the Prime Meridian, delineated by meridians and measured in degrees and minutes of arc.

1 minute = 1 nautical mile only along the Equator due to convergence of meridians as they approach the poles.

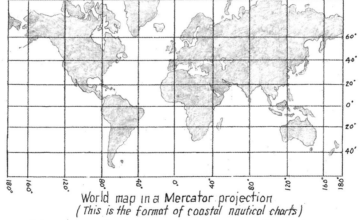

World map in a Mercator projection
(This is the format of coastal nautical charts)

Distances in nautical miles are to be taken off with dividers only in the latitude scale on right and left-hand sides of the chart.

International Date Line. So, for example, where I live in Maine, on Peaks Island, the longitude is 70° 11' West. The longitude of Barcelona, where I was born, is 2° 6' East.

Put latitude and longitude together and you can describe the exact location of any spot on earth to the utmost detail—degrees, minutes, and seconds—although most charts list degrees and minutes and instead of seconds (of which there are sixty per minute) they offer tenths of minutes. It's just an easier calculation to make. Now you are prepared to describe every cove, point of land, favored anchorage, or exotic destination, in its latitude and longitude.

Peaks Island, Maine (that exotic land), therefore, is described as being at 43° 40' North; 70° 11' West. Even if you never heard of Peaks Island, you should still be able to conjure in your mind which quadrant of the globe this place is located in since you can visualize its distance west of the Prime Meridian (about two-fifths of the way around to the Date Line), and visualize its position relative to the Equator and North Pole (not quite halfway to the Pole).

One tricky aspect of navigating in the western hemisphere is the fact that you have to remember that degrees of longitude *increase* as you move west, which can be counterintuitive if you are accustomed to reading left to right (as most of us non-Hebrew readers are). A quick glance at the numbers on the bottom or top of the chart will set you straight, but it's an easy trap to fall into and will get you very lost if you forget.

Once you understand the earth's grid system as put down on a nautical chart, you're ready to start figuring how to move around within it.

DIVIDERS

Tools of the coastal navigator —

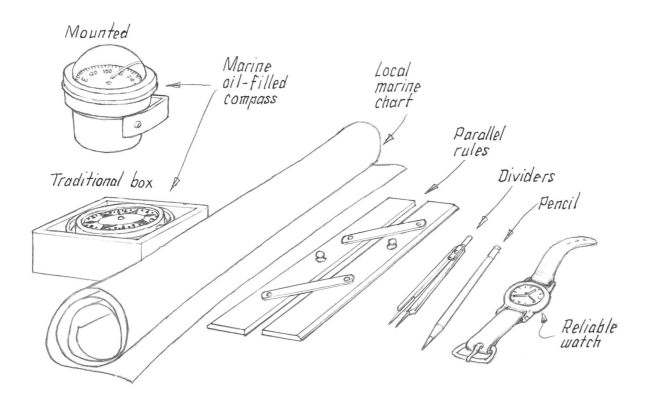

Mounted

Marine oil-filled compass

Local marine chart

Parallel rules

Dividers

Pencil

Traditional box

Reliable watch

Navigational dividers in their simplest form are two metal points that can be expanded or brought together to measure distance, like a pair of calipers. You might measure the distance on the scale of the chart and compare the fixed distance, say, one mile, to the distance you have to travel. Or you might spread the dividers over the total distance and bring that span over the to the chart's scale. The point is that you need something that's adjustable up to about six inches. Some dividers have a metal point on one end and a pencil lead on the other. This is a handy feature when you want to scribe an arc of a given distance off a point of land. If you know, by radar, for example, that you're four miles off a given peninsula, you set the dividers to four miles, put the metal point on the peninsula, and then swing the pencil lead in an arc. You know your position is somewhere on this drawn arc. Or you triangulate a position using three such distances.

PARALLEL RULES

If dividers measure distance, parallel rules calculate direction. And to do this requires orientation on the chart. First is the grid itself. As described earlier, on a Mercator projection chart, the longitude lines run parallel to one another just as the lines of latitude are. The latitude lines run east-west, while the longitude lines run north-south. Remember, this is true direction. If you are sailing due north on your magnetic compass you are not sailing parallel with the longitude lines on the chart; rather, you're sailing along an oblique angle to them. This difference, as stated above, is the variation. To accommodate this difference in direction you need to consult the "compass rose," the two circles drawn in various locations on the chart. The outer circle is true direction; the inner one is magnetic direction. And printed inside is the annual change in variation. Annual change is not significant in most coastal waters of the Lower 48—usually not enough to calculate. If you're using a chart from the 1960s, though, the difference could be significant. What will be most significant (and dangerous), however, is the fact that all of the buoys on the chart will have long since been repainted, renumbered, or repositioned. So you need a relatively recent chart. Even if you have one that's ten years old, it may not be useless, however, if you're willing to update it for changes to buoys and lights in your local area. The NGA publishes a "Notice to Mariners" online (they don't publish these on paper anymore), and it is a relatively simple task to match your chart number with the Notice to Mariners and note any changes right on the chart. (In the Merchant Marine, this thankless job—updating all of a ship's charts—is the official province of the vessel's third mate. "Good overtime pay but boring as hell," quipped a friend of mine recently.) An easier way to see whether your dated chart needs corrections is to visit the National Oceanographic and Atmospheric Administration's (NOAA) web site: www.charts.noaa. gov. All charts in the country are available free of charge. The site is a little cumbersome at first, since you have to know the five-digit designation of the chart (Casco Bay, where Peaks Island is, is on chart 13290, for example), but this is easily gathered through any number of search engines.

The Mariner's Compass

The inner rose (graduated in quarter points) is visually easiest for steering.

The outer rose (in degrees) matches those on the charts for laying-out courses and for plotting bearings.

Back to the compass rose. The important thing to consider—every time you consult the rose—is that you use the direction you intend and not unwittingly switch between magnetic and true. I recommend in coastal navigation that you always use the magnetic (inner) rose. (This defies the centuries-old tradition of always plotting in true, but this tradition was based on ocean-going practices where true direction was more relevant, since the star books offer azimuths (direction) calculated in true.)

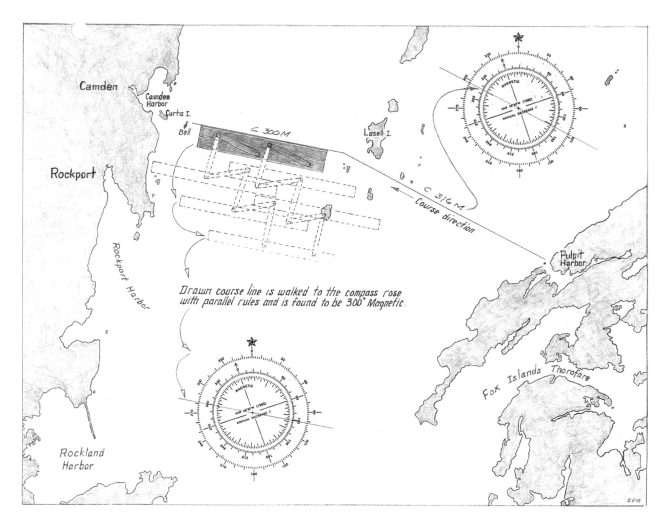

Drawn course line is walked to the compass rose with parallel rules and is found to be 300° Magnetic.

You use a compass rose for two basic reasons: to transfer a known direction *from* the rose to an intended course or bearing, or to do the opposite—determine the numerical compass course of a desired route (or to calculate a bearing) by bringing that angle *to* the compass rose and reading off the numerical direction.

Let's start with determining your course. Let's say *Swallow* is at anchor in Pulpit Harbor on North Haven Island in Maine and you want to know the course to sail back home to Camden. To do so you align your parallel rules so they connect Pulpit Harbor to Camden Harbor. You want to know what direction to steer your boat when you emerge from the harbor so that you ultimately find Camden, some eight miles away and with numerous rocks and islands in the way. A straight line goes through an island, so you actually need two courses, one to the southern tip of Lasell Island, and the next that will take you right to the buoy off Curtis Island in Camden. (I'm simplifying the real course, so don't actually use my numbers for navigation.)

On a small boat such as *Swallow,* you don't have the luxury of a chart table, so the seat will do so long as it is perfectly flat. With the rules laid flat—one end lying at the entrance to Pulpit and the other extending past Lasell along the southern point—"walk" the other leg of the rule toward the compass rose. Do this several times until one edge (it doesn't matter which) lies directly on top of the very center of the rose. Then, read the direction off the inner (magnetic) compass rose in the same direction that you would like to travel—in this case, about 320 degrees. This is your first course. Write it down on a piece of scratch paper with an arrow between the words "Pulpit" and "Lasell." It's a little tricky the first time, but it's pretty simple with practice. The parallel rules have several corks on the bottom so they won't skid on the page. If the rules do skid, you need to start over again. Even a minor slip will drastically change the direction, especially on a course several miles long. Next, place the rules so that they lie with one edge pointing the route between the southern tip of Lasell and Camden Harbor. Repeat the act of walking the rules to the center of the compass rose and read off the next course—about 300 degrees. Write the words "Lasell" and "Camden" with an arrow pointing between the two and note the course. Once you steer out of Pulpit Harbor and past Pulpit rock, you can adjust your course to 320 degrees, trim your sails accordingly, and follow your compass across the bay toward Lasell. Once you arrive there—in GPS speak this is called a "waypoint"—you alter course 20 degrees to the left, to 300 degrees, and you will soon arrive at Camden Harbor, provided the wind holds. It's as simple as that.

Sometimes you'll need to do this in reverse. You might not be able to sail exactly in the desired direction if you don't have a favorable wind, for example. In which case you might have to start at the compass rose with a direction you think you can sail, and then walk the rules over to your known position to see where that course will take you. But it's really the same exercise—matching the direction of the compass rose with your intended course.

BEARING

The compass rose is also necessary for taking "bearings" of known geographical features such as points of land, lighthouses, buoys, or tall buildings that might be labeled on a chart. A bearing is an object's compass direction in relation to your position. (This is not to be confused with "heading," which is the direction in which the boat is pointing at any given time, whether at anchor or underway.)

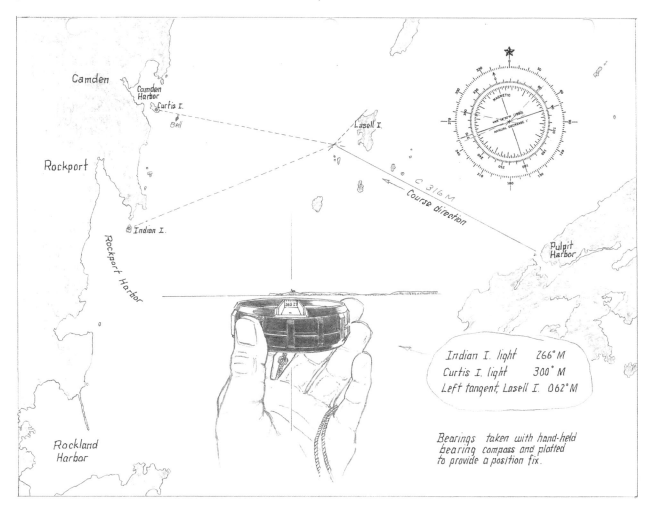

Indian I. light   266° M
Curtis I. light   300° M
Left tangent, Lasell I. 062° M

Bearings taken with hand-held bearing compass and plotted to provide a position fix.

To determine the bearing of an object, stand over your compass so that the compass is positioned between you and the object you're sighting. By sighting over the compass and squinting your eyes in a sailorly way and extending your arm in a kind of karate chop toward the object you can read the direction of the object off the compass. This is that object's bearing. Let's say it's a lighthouse and it bears 170 degrees. This doesn't mean anything to you until you consider this information on the chart. Place the parallel rules so that one edge passes through the center of the compass rose. Next, rotate the rules until the same edge passes through 170 degrees. Then, walk the rules down until one of the edges passes through the lighthouse you were just squinting at. If you draw a faint pencil line on the chart, you can see the actual line you were just describing with your chopping hand motion. Your boat's position is somewhere on this line. You don't know exactly where, but you know you're on it somewhere.

A single line of position (LOP) is handy, but several lines give you what every navigator craves: a "fix." A fix is position that triangulates several bearings to create a known location. A true fix is no fewer than three bearings, the idea being that only by adding a third line do you know for sure that this is your proper location. The third LOP is a measure of redundancy.

WATCH OR CLOCK

When Joshua Slocum sailed from Boston, he did so without a chronometer.

"The want of a chronometer for the voyage was all that now worried me," he wrote. "In our newfangled notions of navigation it is supposed that a mariner cannot find his way without one; and I had myself drifted into this way of thinking. My old chronometer, a good one, had been long in disuse. It would cost fifteen dollars to clean and rate it. Fifteen dollars!"

Instead of paying the $15 he sailed across the Gulf of Maine for Yarmouth, Nova Scotia, and arrived without incident, notwithstanding his lack of timepiece. And there he found the perfect clock.

"At Yarmouth, too, I got my famous tin clock, the only timepiece I carried on the whole voyage, The price of it was a dollar and a half, but on account of the face being smashed the merchant let me have it for a dollar."

This famous clock, an E.N. Welch model called Little Lord Fauntleroy, is a charming little clock that is now a collector's item. But at the time, it was a dime-store trinket. And that was perhaps the whole point.

"He used the tin clock to belittle the contemporary trend toward reliance on technology," wrote Richard SantaCaloma in a 2002 piece about Slocum's clock in the magazine *Ocean Navigator*. "Slocum wanted to show the world how an old salt could do the impossible and with less equipment than thought necessary for a far shorter foray, with far fewer crew. Slocum's clock was symbolic of his disdain for the way the world was going."

This is the same spirit to bring toward all your navigational toolbox items, including a watch. Simpler is better. I prefer an analog watch, since I can visualize the hour in its wholeness and, at the same time, visualize the parts of the hour. Moving at six knots, for example, I can see each ten-minute interval during which I have traveled one knot.

For coastal piloting, a watch is a constant check on progress. If you calculate your speed in advance, you can continuously check progress as you pass buoys or other charted features. In the fog or darkness, of course, a watch is even more essential.

A NOTE ABOUT RADAR

Most small boats do not have radar. There are several reasons for this. First, they require considerable wiring between the antenna, which must be placed high in the rig, and the display, which is usually in the cockpit or below in the nav station, and the batteries. The second reason is that radar takes a lot of juice to operate, so suddenly you exponentially increase the complexity of the vessel's systems. Instead of an engine turning only a propeller, you also need it to charge a large battery bank. If you have a large battery bank, you might as well have cabin lights, and, while you're at it, a small 12-volt plug for your laptop computer. And so on. Electricity is a drug and is very addictive. So I advocate an electricity-free boat. You really can have a small boat—*Swallow* is just twenty feet long—with only an engine and two deep-cycle batteries, one for starting the engine and the other for powering the running lights. In fact, while we designed *Swallow* with an engine, the only reason we did was so we could discuss maneuvering under power. The ideal *Swallow* in my eyes would not have an engine at all—just a long pair of "sweeps" (oars) for moving the boat along when the wind dies.

But *if* you're seduced by the allure of electricity and *if* you end up with a battery bank large enough to accommodate a small radar set, I would advocate the purchase of radar over any other electronic device, even a GPS. This is because only radar can do what you can't: see through the dark or fog and give you a picture of what's *actually* out there. GPS only tells you what *should* be where the chart says it is. Radar, on the other hand, tells you if there are passing or anchored ships in your vicinity, and it tells you the shape of the land or any other hard object in relation to your position.

There are two main reasons for radar: navigation and collision avoidance. For navigational purposes, radar offers you two measurements: bearing relative to your boat's location and heading and distance (from your boat and between other objects).

Collision avoidance by radar is a function of tracking other targets (boats) and determining whether, if each vessel maintains its course and speed, there is risk of collision. This is called tracking another vessel's CPA (closest point of approach). You perform this function by taking timed snapshots of targets on your radar and comparing them to one another over a short period of time—say, in six-minute increments (six minutes equals one-tenth of an hour, making math calculations simple). Accordingly, it is essential to observe radar targets early enough that you can allow the scenario to unfold long enough to predict whether a close-quarters situation exists.

There are plenty of good books on the subject of radar navigation, the best of which is likely your radar set's owner's manual, and the subject is too vast to explore in any detail here for our purposes. But if you take the time to learn how to do a basic CPA plot and basic navigational fixes (lines of position combined with distances), radar will be your navigational best friend.

6

ANCHORING, MOORING, & DOCKING

"An anchor works like a pick axe. When the pick is driven into the ground, it would require a tremendous amount of force to pull it loose with a straight pull on the handle. By lifting the handle, however, a leverage is obtained which breaks it free. In the same way, an anchor holds because a long cable causes the pull on the anchor to be in line with the shank."

—from *The American Merchant's Seaman's Manual*

My first command was an engineless wooden ketch about twenty-eight feet long. I had a crew of six young people who were learning the basics of seamanship on the Maine coast on a three-week cruise. We sailed from island to island, spending our days navigating amongst the shoals and bays of Eastern Maine. The boat was too small to sleep aboard comfortably; in fact, there was no cabin at all, and each evening we would anchor the boat, haul our gear ashore in the dinghy, and set up our tents in a patch of grass on a different deserted island. It was a blissful summer.

One afternoon we were approaching an anchorage near Spruce Head, Maine. The approach required a westerly course of about a mile and a final turn into a protected cove on the northern shore of the island. We would anchor in about ten feet of water at a

An anchoring experience

spot that was close to the beach. It was late in the day so the setting sun was in our faces as we ghosted along in the fading breeze. I hauled out the fisherman anchor, picking it up in my arms—it weighed about twenty-five pounds—and stood on the little foredeck to scout our anchorage. I gave periodic instructions to the helmsman to change course a few degrees one way or the other, turning slightly each time so that my voice could be heard. The dew had started to fall, and I noticed, too late, that the decks were slippery beneath my rubber boots. The next moment I slipped over the rail and fell flat on my back into the water—the anchor still clutched to my chest. What happened next was slow motion in my mind—I remember each instant with absolute clarity—yet likely it only took two seconds in actual time.

The anchor pushed me underwater, as did the weight of the length of chain that was attached to its ring, and the boat sailed on—her startled crew in a stunned trance. I remember looking up at the surface of the water from about ten feet below the surface and realizing I was about to die a very stupid death unless I could free myself immediately. I can still picture the tangle of Nylon line, darkly silhouetted against the sparkling water, snaking swiftly over the side above me as I shot to the bottom of the sea. I must have dumped the anchor in an instant, since I popped to the surface in time to grab the stern of the boat just before she slipped away.

I hauled myself aboard in a soggy heap and collapsed in the bottom of the cockpit. The crew gaped at me at their feet, their once-proud skipper an ignominious lump of wet clothing. I was uninjured. I recall recovering my humor enough to mumble something about the need for graceful anchoring maneuvers at the end of a long day of sailing. My approach was as graceless (and dangerous) as they come. But grace really is the point to a successful anchoring or docking maneuver. You should be able to envision each maneuver in your mind beforehand—picture how the boat will swing into position, the lines will be handled, who will handle them, and how you want the boat to lie once it comes to a complete stop. Sea literature is filled with these beautiful maneuvers.

Consider Sterling Hayden's extraordinary docking of *Wanderbird* upon his return from Tahiti into a narrow berth in Sausalito. With a strong ebb current sweeping past two piers, Hayden must choose between anchoring offshore—effectively chickening out—and maneuvering cross-current to slip into his berth between the piers. Ever the showman, Hayden obviously opts to work his way into the narrow slot, perpendicular to the current's flow. He drives the schooner upcurrent, just past the slot to starboard, and then does a quick back-and-fill maneuver by putting the helm hard over to port and alternately revving the big diesel full astern and then full ahead in short bursts. The big, full-keeled schooner swings in a wide arc. With the schooner now oriented almost parallel with its berth but still upcurrent, Hayden presses the throttle to full astern as the mate, Spike Africa, orders stern lines ashore.

"She pounds in, stern first, threading the eye of the slot," Hayden writes. "In an off-hand manner, Spike slips a line down on the neck of a passing piling. 'Fourteen inches,' he says, 'fourteen inches to spare.'"

Hayden proceeds to claw his way into the berth with a spring line, the mate "checking" (making fast) and "surging" (easing in quick bursts) the various lines until *Wanderbird* is lying neatly alongside. "I ring down with a vengeance: 'Finished with engines!'"

The scene is graceful, has a hint of danger, and is just a little macho—as all the best docking maneuvers are. It was vintage Sterling Hayden.

THE RIGHT ANCHOR

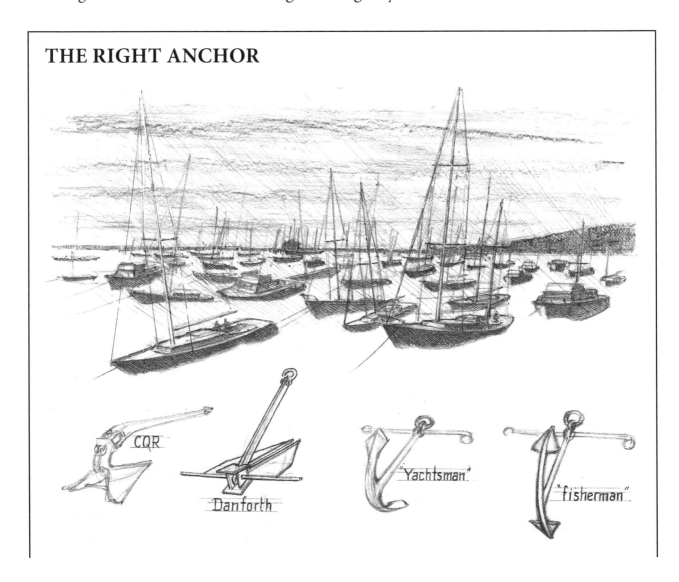

The illustration on p.118 was made in the aftermath of the 60-knot gale which lashed Cuttyhunk I. in Buzzards Bay for 24 hours on July 4 and 5, 1978. The drawing was made to accompany a story in the **National Fisherman**.

How well does an anchor hold?
Sometimes there's opportunity for comparison.

My wife and I, camp-cruising in our 19' banks dory , had pulled into Cuttyhunk harbor on Monday night of that mid-week holiday. The place was filled to overflowing with pleasure boats long-weekending there and anchored closely together for lack of rentable moorings. Fireworks shot off by exhuberant townspeople throughout the evening disguised the dark approach of a violent storm which blew from the east later that night, all day Tuesday and early Wednesday. A few of the larger yachts escaped to deal with the gale in open water. The remainder thrashed at short-stay over weed-entangled bottom. Many dragged into oneanother. A few became beached. As the storm subsided Wednesday morning Susan and I rowed from yacht to yacht with the greeting, "National Fisherman. What kind of groundtackle did you have down and how well did it hold?" Here's a summary of the answers we obtained from the boats that hadn't departed:

Type	Held	Dragged
CQR	5	1
Danforth	27	5
Yachtsman	1	1
Fisherman		4
(info. incomplete)	5	
	38	11

The 49 boats queried had crew aboard throughout the storm. Most were sailing craft. The variables of scope and chain-addition (or not) to the rode were not consistent in the holding or dragging of these anchors. Depth of mud and the array of anchor-choking sticks, shells and weed appears to have governed the holding power at each site.

Sam Manning

There is no such thing as a right anchor for all conditions; the choice of an anchor is subject to the vicissitudes of sea conditions, the geography and weather of the surrounding landscape, and the topography of the sea floor. And there are certainly *wrong* anchors. In *The Compleat Cruiser*, one of Herreshoff's fictional skippers humiliates himself attempting to prove the superiority of a newfangled stockless anchor he had recently purchased. As his crew and friends looked on, Weldon attempted to set the anchor numerous times, even reverting to loading it with additional weight in a vain attempt to get it to set. Each attempt failed, and he grew more and more frustrated as his *Rozinante* continued to drag. He threw out more and more "rode" (anchor line) to increase the scope, only to find that each time the bow rose up on the crest of a wave that the line would come up taught and jerk the anchor free again. He finally admitted defeat, unshackled the anchor from the anchor rode, and hopped into his dinghy with the anchor. He rowed away from *Rozinante* and heaved the anchor overboard. "To the bottom I pitch it!" he shouted. And rowed back to his boat.

"Why did you do that?" his friend Goddard asked. "You might have sold it for junk."

"Yes, I know," Weldon said, "but I would hate to think that some unsuspecting person might get it and lose his boat or even his life with such an anchor."

Weldon and Goddard preferred a traditional anchor with a perpendicular stock—the cross-arm of the centuries-old anchor design, the kind Popeye has tattooed on each forearm. This timeless design is flawless in its simplicity. The anchor lies on the bottom in such a way that it cannot help digging one of its flukes into the bottom. The stock functions to keep the crown lying flat on the bottom and the flukes positioned perpendicular to the bottom. The weight of the chain and the occasional tug on the rode only serve to dig it deeper into the bottom.

A friend of mine once called his old-fashioned anchor (also called a Fisherman's or an Old Fashioned anchor) his "sleeping pill." He'd throw it over the side and know he'd get a good night's sleep—not lie awake all night wondering if his anchor was dragging.

Which is not to say modern stockless anchors don't have a place. Stockless anchors are far easier to handle on deck, since they can be stored easily on a bow roller; they can be laid almost perfectly flat on deck. I know I would not have fallen overboard handling a stockless anchor, since I could have suspended it above the water, one hand on the rode, without it banging clumsily against the hull as we sailed along. I had to hold the traditional anchor in my arms because the boat was not equipped with a "cathead" to keep it free of the hull. And there are numerous designs—flat-fluked Danforth anchors, the plow-shaped CQR (say it fast and it sounds like "secure"), and Bruce anchors—but they require careful attention to the local conditions mentioned above. The best way to choose an anchor is to walk the docks at your local boatyard and ask others what holds well on the bottom. I've found that stockless anchors typically require a whole lot more line than a traditional anchor, the idea being that you want the pull on the anchor to be virtually parallel to the bottom. This means that you often need a depth-to-rode ratio (the "scope") of more than five-to-one. (The length of anchor rode you pay out being five times more than the water's depth. In just thirty feet of water, even five-to-one means 180 feet of anchor rode! Some anchors require up to eight- or even ten-to-one, especially in an anchorage with a swell or a modest chop.)

A traditional anchor will actually set quite well with the scope at just a 45-degree angle—or a ratio of only two-to-one. Weldon summed up his feelings for stockless anchors thus: "I see no earthly reason why they should be used on small craft."

Whatever your choice, *Swallow* is equipped with a traditional anchor. It can be slung casually on the rail and lashed into place, provided you're not too fussy about the bright-work on the rail and the chafing the hull might get in the bow beneath the anchor. Many smaller traditional anchors even come apart—the stock pulling free from the shank—so that the anchor can be stored perfectly flat, either on deck or in a locker.

I will say that stockless anchors are much easier to handle. Many boats I have sailed on have them fitted to a roller on the bow. To drop a stockless anchor on a bow roller is as simple as easing the chain and rode out so that it simply hangs in the vertical position. Easing it a little at a time, once the boat comes to a complete stop, is a cinch. You barely have to touch the anchor except to get it free of the bow roller. The last thing I'd like to add about the differences between anchor styles is that I have shared numerous anchorages with boats of all kinds. When I have been on a boat equipped with a traditional anchor, I have been largely secure in my anchorages, regardless of weather. It is the yachtsmen with the gleaming hulls, their stockless anchors poised for easy handling, who spend a great deal of time setting and resetting their anchors. They don't want the traditional anchors dinging their Gelcoat, but they pay the price when it comes to worry, paying out great lengths of line to increase their scope, and frequently setting and resetting their anchors.

SELECTING AN ANCHORAGE

Selecting an anchorage involves either local knowledge or careful review of the chart—or a combination of both. First, ask the locals about good anchorages. Ask about prevailing conditions. Is there a swell? Is the cove protected from shifting winds? Is it a muddy or sandy bottom or a rocky one? Is there weed or kelp? And then study the chart.

Charts give detailed descriptions of the characteristics of the sea floor. Chart No. 1, a publication produced by (but no longer printed by) the US Government, but available by private companies in book form and ubiquitous online, describes all the symbols on a chart. But, really, all you need to know about a good anchorage can be determined by studying the chart of the area you're sailing in. And once you're at the location you can do your own investigation, either by dropping a lead line (packed with tallow or some other heavy grease in the dimple on the bottom) in the traditional way, or dropping and raising your anchor a few times to see what sticks to it. This can be time consuming (and exhausting), but if you want a good night's rest, it's a worthy exercise.

Lead line —

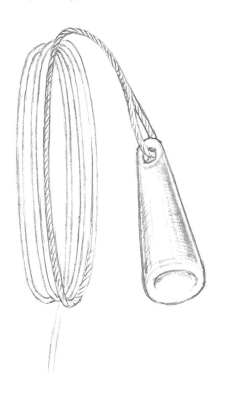

Lead sinker on a fishline with bottom hollowed to hold a lump of tallow or heavy grease for picking up samples of bottom mud, clay, or sediment.

You'll want to consider your forecast in selecting your anchorage. If it's predicted to blow southerly, you'll want an anchorage that has land between you and the prevailing wind. Even if you anchor on the north side of an island, you still might have a swell that wraps around the point and makes for an uncomfortable anchorage. A swell does not necessarily mean you can't stay there, but it does make it less than ideal, especially if you want to hop in your dinghy and unload yourself, your crew, and your gear. So the ideal anchorage is one with a good bottom (not too rocky), is protected from the wind and waves, and offers a short row to a beach, if that's in your plans.

SETTING THE ANCHOR

Let's imagine that we've selected our anchorage and have positioned *Swallow* where it is to be anchored. The boat is essentially stopped—no forward motion through the water but maybe has a little sternway, less than half a knot. We would lower the anchor gently over the side until we feel it touch bottom. The line will instantly become lighter without the weight of the anchor. Then, slowly, we pay out the line a little at a time, keeping a modest strain on the anchor line so that the anchor begins to dig into the bottom as we pay out line. And then we stop (when we feel we have enough line out) by taking a turn or two around a bow cleat or the Sampson post. We may want to surge the line a little once we feel a significant strain on the line. Repeat this a few times—surging and checking—to be sure the anchor has set. Then we wait and see if it drags. You can tell an anchor is dragging in a few ways, first by feeling the rode with your hand. If it's slipping you'll likely feel the vibration in the line itself as the anchor skips across rocks or grinds through sand. It feels a little like playing "telephone" with two paper cups and a length of string. The anchor's vibrations—or lack thereof—communicate to you on the surface as you lightly grasp the line in your hand. You can also look around you and see whether you're holding position relative to the land or other anchored boats. If we were planning on spending the night in this spot, I might run the diesel at dead slow astern for a moment or two to simulate the effect of the strain the boat might be subjected to if the wind rises during the night. If it is slipping, you'll want to either release more scope (if you have the room astern) or reset the anchor entirely by raising it up and repeating the process above until you're satisfied it's actually set.

Since *Swallow* is equipped with a traditional anchor, I likely wouldn't go to great lengths to ensure a proper set, especially if we were anchored in mud or sand in reasonably fair weather. With a scope of about three- or four-to-one in a protected anchorage, this is as good as anchoring gets. It's time to crack open a beer and start telling stories about the day's adventures.

USING A SENTINEL

One way to increase your scope without paying out more anchor rode is to drop a "sentinel" about halfway down the length of your rode. You might do this if you don't have enough room to pay out the necessary line. By dropping a weight—a second anchor, for

Setting the anchor —

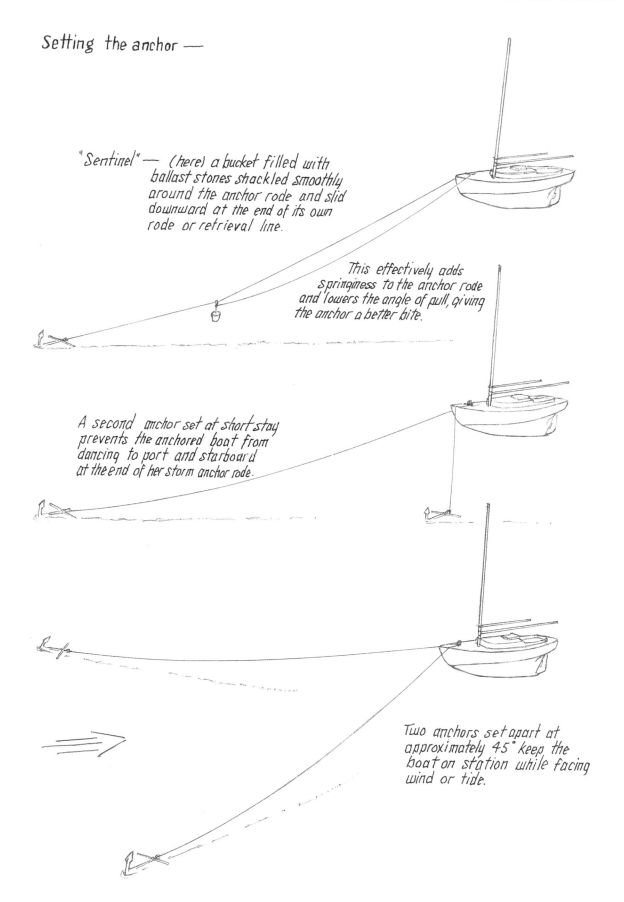

"Sentinel" — (here) a bucket filled with ballast stones shackled smoothly around the anchor rode and slid downward at the end of its own rode or retrieval line.

This effectively adds springiness to the anchor rode and lowers the angle of pull, giving the anchor a better bite.

A second anchor set at short stay prevents the anchored boat from dancing to port and starboard at the end of her storm anchor rode.

Two anchors set apart at approximately 45° keep the boat on station while facing wind or tide.

example—down the anchor rode you force the rode to lie at a shallower angle between the sentinel and the anchor on the bottom. To do this you anchor normally with the boat's primary anchor and then send the second anchor, shackled around the primary anchor's rode, down on its own rode.

Adding a sentinel has the added benefit of acting like an elastic band against a swell. The downward weight on the anchor rode counteracts the upward effect of a swell pushing up on the bow. But this is one of those tricks that looks good in an illustration and makes intuitive sense to a crafty Yankee sailor but in practice seems only like a last-ditch effort. Yet it might work and is certainly worth a try in a tight anchorage that also has a nasty swell.

ROUGH WEATHER ANCHORING

I was once anchored in a cove off of Islesboro, Maine, riding out the last effects of a tropical storm. The boat was an old wooden schooner and was equipped with two enormous iron anchors, one weighing about 400 pounds (the storm anchor) and the other, our "working anchor" (for daily use), was about two-thirds the weight. It was blowing a steady twenty-five knots in the afternoon, meaning we had a double reef in the main and were sailing under just the foresail and forestaysail. The jib stayed tightly furled to the bowsprit all day. The storm was predicted to build during the night to about forty-five knots before it petered out by morning. The anchorage offered plenty of protection from the northeast and was also reasonably protected from the northwest should the "clearing wind" fill in early in the morning. I dropped the storm anchor and then, once we were satisfied with the amount of chain we released, I dropped the working anchor straight down with just enough scope so that the anchor was lying flat on the bottom.

The idea was to prevent the schooner from "sailing" back and forth on its single anchor. A boat on its anchor or mooring in a gale of wind will scoot back and forth as the wind catches one side of the bow, pushing it off in one direction until the anchor rode draws it up tight. Then it jerks suddenly, pivoting at the bow, the bow and the stern swinging around, so that the wind then catches the other side of the hull and sends the boat sailing off in the other direction. Back and forth, each time tugging violently on the anchor and—potentially—causing it to drag. At the very least, even if the boat does not drag, the motion can cause considerable damage to the hawsepipe, the "headrig" (bobchain, whisker stays, and footropes), and even the cleat or post the anchor rode is attached to. By dropping this second anchor straight down, you arrest this motion before it gets a chance to happen. The boat never gets a chance to start sailing off at an oblique angle; it stays roughly where it is.

This worked remarkably well. We kept an eye on the anchors through the night, posting a rotating anchor watch every hour to be sure we did not drag or otherwise foul our anchors. By morning the storm had blown out, and, other than having to work the hand-cranked windlass to haul two anchors instead of one, we got underway in a beautiful northwest breeze that carried us home.

There's another way to effectively use two anchors during rough weather—by dropping one off the port bow and the other off the starboard bow. Each anchor ends up at roughly a 45-degree angle from the centerline of the boat. This effectively cuts in half the strain on each anchor, improving the hold considerably and therefore diminishing the chances of dragging. To position two anchors in this position, you drop one first and then maneuver the boat, either by sails or engine or some combination of both, so that you end up veering across the wind to the second anchor's position. As you're maneuvering, you're also paying out rode on the first anchor. After dropping the second anchor, you then haul half the rode of the first anchor back on board, while paying out the rode of the second, until the bow of the vessel lies equidistant between each anchor. (You can also accomplish this same anchor-positioning arrangement by carrying out an anchor in a dinghy, as explained below.)

Dropping two anchors might also be favorable in a crowded anchorage in which swinging with the tide may not be desirable. To do this, you position a windward anchor and a leeward anchor. You drop the windward anchor first, and then, while drifting astern with the wind, pay out twice the length you need before dropping the leeward anchor. You then take up half the length of the windward-anchor rode while paying out rode on the leeward anchor. There is no strain on the leeward anchor at all until the tide (or wind) shifts, at which point the strain switches from one to the next. This can be a hell of a clumsy affair if the lines become crossed. My *American Merchant Seaman's Manual* goes on for several pages about how to unfoul a pair of crossed and tangled anchor chains. All I can say is that it's not worth it. If the anchorage seems too crowded and does not offer ample room to swing with the tide, find another anchorage unless you're darned sure you can keep your lines from fouling. One very simply way to keep a pair of anchor lines from fouling around one another is to drop one anchor off the stern. This is easy and can be accomplished as above or using a dinghy. You have to be careful not to end up at the bottom of the sea while handling an anchor in a dinghy (as I almost did), but with a little caution it can be accomplished easily enough. The idea is to avoid placing the anchor into the dinghy at all; rather, if you lash its ring to the rail of the dinghy with the anchor hanging, flukes down, into the water, you eliminate the risk of being carried over the side in a tangle of line. You can unlash the anchor when you're ready and pay out the anchor rode slowly as the anchor descends to the bottom.

MOORING ALONGSIDE

We can't all be Sterling Hayden in our docking maneuvers, macho and graceful and masterful. Yet, with a little practice, we can at least have his skill in anticipating the motion of our boat when it comes in close contact with a dock. You do this with practice. I was once training a young, female captain how to maneuver a schooner into a tight berth that required a last-minute jog around a set of pilings. I instructed her to anticipate the attitude of the approach on various tides. An ebb tide would set her forcefully down onto the dock, while the flood would push her away. The ebb tide, therefore, required a more nimble and nuanced approach, since too much speed would cause a violent crash, while the flood required her to be more aggressive and use higher rpm to force the schooner alongside, against the tide. She practiced the approach dozens of times—working in sync with the deckhands to cast docking lines ashore at the right time and in the right sequence, until she'd built sufficient confidence that she could manage the schooner on her own with a full load of passengers.

Nothing I offered prepared her for one of her first solo docking maneuvers, however. She was coming in on the flood tide, meaning she had to come into the berth "hot," with a fair amount of speed through the water. Just as she was making the final turn of the wheel, having shifted into astern propulsion and pressed the rpm up to half speed, a spoke of the helm caught her blouse, tearing open her shirt—in full view of her passengers and dozens of onlookers on the dock. She was faced with an immediate choice: cover herself in modesty (and risk botching the maneuver) or dock the boat with grace. She chose the latter, and the schooner slipped alongside as neatly as a seasoned professional. The passengers cheered.

And that's how it is with docking boats. Just as you gain a measure of confidence, something crazy and unexpected happens. So you might as well practice again and again so the maneuver itself becomes second nature.

Docking under power ——

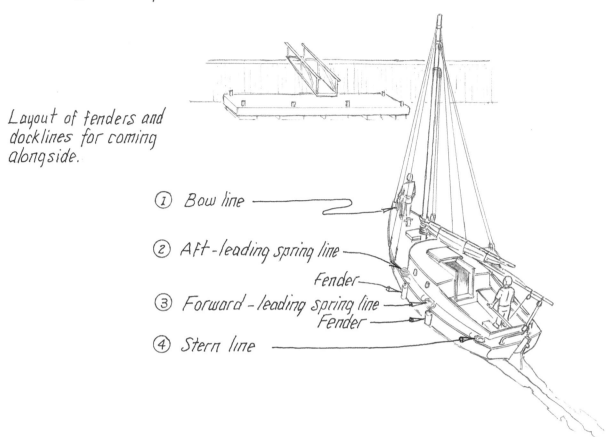

Layout of fenders and docklines for coming alongside.

① Bow line

② Aft-leading spring line

Fender

③ Forward-leading spring line

Fender

④ Stern line

Following is a description of how to maneuver *Swallow* alongside a dock—portside-to. We'll assume there's negligible effect from wind and tide. We'll want to approach the dock at a 45-degree angle or slightly less. It's actually quite difficult to maneuver a boat alongside a dock from a narrow angle. You want to take advantage of the side-slipping motion that comes from putting the helm down and backing the engine. (Imagine skidding into a parking place like Starsky and Hutch.) But first, picture the lines you'll want to have in place once you're moored neatly alongside. You want four lines in most docking scenarios: a stern line, which I always call the Number 4 line and runs straight out from the boat, leading somewhat aft onto the dock; a bow line, which I call the Number 1 and leads at a slight angle forward from the bow to the dock; and two spring lines, which will keep the boat from slipping either astern or forward once the boat is positioned alongside. The after-leading spring is the Number 2 (since it's the second line you encounter as you walk aft on deck), and the forward-leading spring line is the Number 3. It's best if the spring lines cross one another as they lead to the dock. This gives them the most length as compared to the length of the boat. Spring lines are aptly named, since they can be used to spring alongside a dock or spring off a dock. The longer the line, the easier it is to use as leverage. But I'm getting ahead of myself.

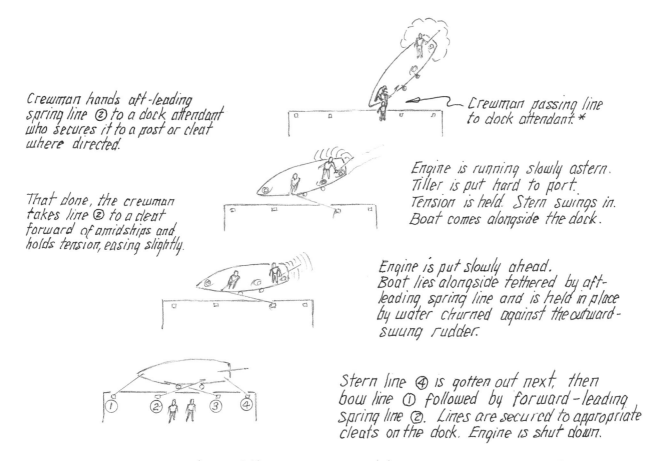

Crewman hands aft-leading spring line ② to a dock attendant who secures it to a post or cleat where directed.

That done, the crewman takes line ② to a cleat forward of amidships and holds tension, easing slightly.

Crewman passing line to dock attendant.*

Engine is running slowly astern. Tiller is put hard to port. Tension is held. Stern swings in. Boat comes alongside the dock.

Engine is put slowly ahead. Boat lies alongside tethered by aft-leading spring line and is held in place by water churned against the outward-swung rudder.

Stern line ④ is gotten out next, then bow line ① followed by forward-leading spring line ②. Lines are secured to appropriate cleats on the dock. Engine is shut down.

* If no crewman or dock attendant is available, the skipper reaches out and drops the loop-end of springline ② over the the dockside cleat or bollard. He then takes up the inboard end of ② routed around the forward-of-amidships cleat as before, and holds tension with one hand while handling the tiller with the other.

Next, place each line on deck in roughly the place you'll want them to end up once they're secured. Each dock line should have a loop—either a bowline tied in place or a spliced eye—on one end. That is the end that will go to the dock. The other end you and your crew will adjust from the deck of the boat. You don't want some stranger, a dockhand or someone from another boat, adjusting the tension on the line as it's thrown to them. You want them to not have to think, just place the eye around the cleat that is nearest to them. You are responsible for your boat and your crew and can instruct them how and when to take up or slack the lines from the deck. Who knows what an unskilled stranger will do to sabotage your perfect landing, and it's a good idea to think of everyone other than your own crew as not to be trusted with the tense moments involved in docking. Next, imagine the fenders you need in position. Probably at least two, positioned on either side of the beamiest part of the boat. Secure them on their cleats well in advance of the approach. While it is unsailorly to sail around with your fenders hanging overboard, you don't want to be fumbling with them in the final seconds of your approach.

Lastly, go over with your crew what you're envisioning for an approach: which lines will go where, whether someone should step off the dock to take lines ashore, and which line you want secured first. Aboard *Swallow* I would ask that the after-leading spring line—the Number 2—be the first to be secured to the dock. By sending that line ashore and instructing a deckhand to take a turn around a cleat and apply tension, you can then *walk* the boat alongside. You don't want to stop short with this line. If you do, the bow will immediately pivot toward the dock, and you will crash into it. Rather, you want gentle tension, easing (surging) the line as it comes up taught so that the boat's forward motion is arrested at the same time that, with the tiller hard over to port and the engine running slowly astern, the stern slides easily alongside. Then the rest of the lines can go over to the dock, first the stern line (Number 4), and then the bow (Number 1) and forward-leading spring (Number 3). The reason for this order is that you maintain the control of the boat at all times. With just the Number 2 (after-leading) spring line attached to the dock, you can keep the boat alongside by idling the engine slowly ahead and keeping the tiller hard over to port. The motion of the water streaming from the propeller past the rudder keeps the stern tucked against the dock, while the spring line keeps the boat from making any forward way. In this arrangement you can slip the three remaining lines ashore at your leisure.

Once the boat is safely alongside, place "locking" hitches on all the dock lines, double-check your fenders so that they do not ride up onto the dock and allow the hull to contact the dock, and secure your engine. If you practice this maneuver a dozen times, you are well on your way to becoming nimble in what is arguably one of the most fun and (occasionally) exciting maneuvers you can have on a boat.

GETTING UNDERWAY

To prepare to get underway, rehearse in your mind which lines will be under strain. Do you want the bow to swing out? If so, you will reverse the engine and back on the forward-leading spring line, line Number 3. All the other lines (1, 2, and 4) can come aboard immediately. If you want the stern to swing out, you will engage the engine ahead and spring off line Number 2, the after-leading spring line. Then tell your crew what

Getting underway when docked port-side-to —

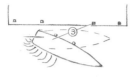

To swing the bow out, reverse the engine and back down on ③ the forward-leading spring line. Drop the remaining lines ① ② and ④. Move fenders to where they are effective.

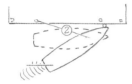

To swing the stern out, run the engine forward and spring off on line ② the aft-leading spring line.

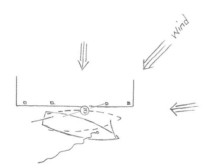

To swing off under sail with wind from, or along, the dock, back the jib, loose the main and spring off the dock on line ③, the forward-leading spring, if necessary.

you envision so they know what to expect. Be sure to place fenders in the positions that the hull will come to bear against the dock. Once underway, stow all your fenders and remove all the dock lines from the deck so they are not a tripping hazard.

You can get underway from a dock using the sails, provided the winds are favorable. If it's blowing you directly onto the dock, it simply cannot be done safely. However, if it's blowing parallel to the dock or in any angle off the dock, getting underway is a breeze! Just consider where your center of effort is when you put up each sail. Putting up the jib and backing it will force the bow away from the dock if you keep the main slack and luffing. Sailing onto and off a dock is thrilling and is a vestige of a time when engines were not considered a necessity. I've sailed onto and off docks on vessels ranging from ten feet to 100 feet and each time is slightly different, exciting in its own way. Talking through the maneuver beforehand and speaking clearly during its execution are the keys to success.

7

SAILING GEAR

"No prudent master, however peaceably inclined, would go to sea without his pistols and handcuffs."

—from *Two Years Before the Mast*, by Richard Henry Dana

When Sterling Hayden sailed away from San Francisco aboard the schooner *Wanderbird*, spiriting away his four children against a court order, he did so in angry defiance. Trapped by the phoniness of his Hollywood life, cornered by the law, and driven almost to insolvency by his expensive divorce, Hayden saw his chance to recover the carefree adventure of his youth. The sea beckoned. All he had to do was slip the lines from the wharf and sail away through the Golden Gate. Which is what he did, embarking on a 4,000-mile voyage to Papeete with his children and a ragtag band of schooner hooligans—including a burly chief mate named Spike Africa.

"What does a man need—really need?" Hayden wrote in his 1963 memoir *Wanderer*. "A few pounds of food each day, heat and shelter, six feet to lie down in—and some form of working activity that will yield a sense of accomplishment. That's all—in the material sense. And we know it."

Bilge pumps —

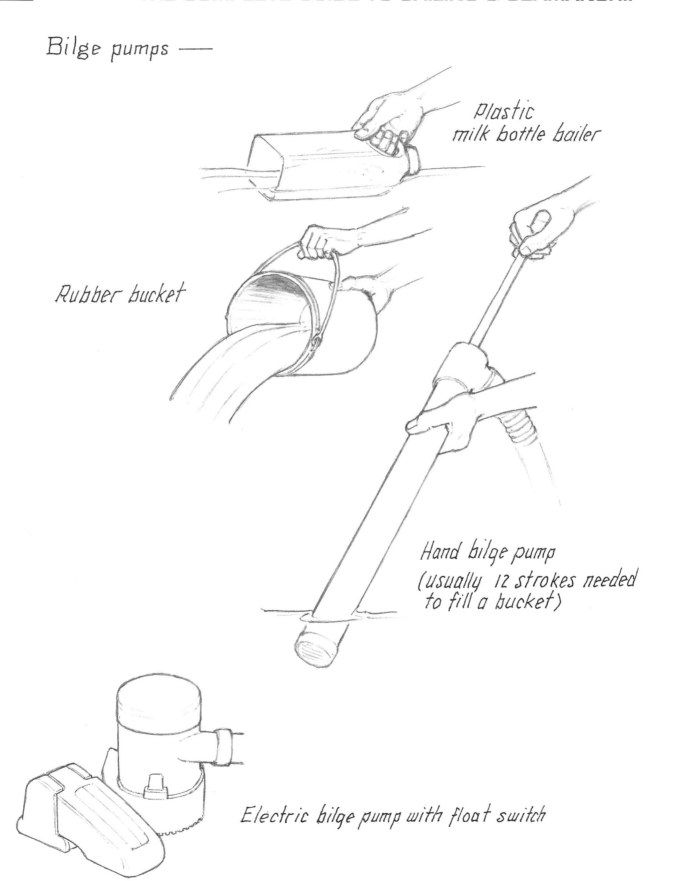

Plastic
milk bottle bailer

Rubber bucket

Hand bilge pump
(usually 12 strokes needed
to fill a bucket)

Electric bilge pump with float switch

He arrived in Tahiti and held out for months, exchanging angry telegrams with lawyers and Hollywood agents until he brokered a fragile peace that allowed him to return with his dignity and the prospect of a lucrative book deal. (He also must have had an exceedingly patient ex-wife who likely trusted him enough with their children to know he just needed to blow steam for a while.) Yet there is an alluring simplicity to Hayden's sailing spirit that is as meaningful today as it was prescient and important at the time. He continued:

"But we are brainwashed by our economic system until we end up in a tomb beneath a pyramid of time payments, mortgages, preposterous gadgetry, playthings that divert our attention from the sheer idiocy of the charade." Hayden was talking about life ashore, but he could have just as easily been describing his view toward sailing and over-gadgeted boats. *Wanderbird* was an old, battered schooner with a monstrous diesel engine and no systems to speak of. An expert celestial navigator from his years as a schooner captain prior to his movie career, Hayden was as self-reliant as he was arrogant. Yet he could afford to thumb his nose at the establishment; his schooner was a self-contained kingdom that could take him anywhere on the high seas.

And then there's Ernest Shackleton. His story remains famous, almost 100 years later, because of the dogged persistence of the leader and the simplicity of its execution. A challenge arose; the group met it head on with dogged determination. I won't repeat the whole story here but instead will focus on only one aspect of the two-year expedition—the open-boat voyage from Elephant Island to South Georgia. In the twenty-two-foot boat *James Caird* was Shackleton, *Endurance*'s skilled captain Frank Worsley, the second mate Thomas Crean, the well-liked and powerfully built Timothy McCarthy, the ship's carpenter Harry McNeish, and the able seaman John Vincent—the last two chosen simply because they were too incorrigible to be left behind on Elephant Island with the rest of the crew. Shackleton took them so he could keep an eye on them.

Shackleton and his crew of five would need to cross the Drake Passage, "the most dreaded bit of ocean on the globe," so that they could report the location of the rest of their party back on Elephant Island and arrange rescue. They had to succeed or their shipmates would be marooned indefinitely on a windswept, rocky beach in the Southern Ocean, surrounded by icebergs.

Prior to departure *James Caird* was crudely decked over with crossbeams and then covered in canvas so that she was entirely sealed against the weather with the exception of a small cockpit aft. Here, the helmsman could crouch at the tiller and look out upon the waves, keep an eye on sail trim, and, at the same time, keep a lookout for icebergs, rushing waves, and any sign of land. The crew shook hands with the shore party and, waist-deep in the icy surf, launched *James Caird* in the backwash of a large wave. The little boat was equipped with a pair of binoculars, a compass, a small medicine chest, four oars, a bailing bucket that doubled as a "hoosh pot" (for mixing their morning concoction of powdered milk, bouillon, and hot water), a hand-built brass bilge pump, a shotgun and shells for killing seabirds for food, a small canvas sea anchor for when the weather became too rough to keep moving, a fishing line, a few candles, several boxes of matches, navigation books (hydrographic tables and nautical almanac), a small tool chest, and lengths of spare rope. (This rope would come in especially handy when the group arrived on the wrong side of South Georgia Island and proceeded to cross overland, through the precipitous mountains to the whaling station that could arrange for a rescue—but that's another story.)

The voyage was nearly 1,000 miles long; it took them three weeks. They battled storm after storm and waves that exceeded fifty feet in height. They were swamped too many times to mention and were soaked through the entire journey, their vessel covered in a kind of hairy slurry, the result of their rotting reindeer-hide sleeping bags. "Reindeer bags in such a hopeless sloppy slimy mess, smelling badly & weighing so heavily that we throw two of the worst overboard," quipped Worsely.

But they made it, arriving at South Georgia Island three weeks later, having crossed almost 1,000 miles of open ocean. The navigation alone was a minor miracle. "They both knew that except for one of two tiny islands, the Atlantic Ocean eastward beyond South Georgia is a void all the way to South Africa, nearly 3,000 miles away," wrote Alfred Lansing in his classic 1959 book, *Endurance*. "If, through a miscalculation or because of a southerly gale, they missed the island, there would be no second chance." Worsley was able to find South Georgia by taking briefly snatched glimpses of sun sights from the tiny cockpit of the storm-tossed cockleshell of a boat and then reducing the sights on the chart by referring, delicately, to the soaked pages of the hydrographic tables and nautical almanac. As the world well remembers, they landed at South Georgia, crossed overland to the whaling station, and set in motion a rescue effort that would last four months. Yet Shackleton secured his reputation as the leader who "never lost a man."

I don't advocate equipping one's boat like *James Caird* for the sake of reliving some of Shackleton's misery; rather, to suggest that if they could cross 1,000 miles of the Drake Passage in a tiny boat and live—if not comfortably, then certainly safely—then one can cruise the coastal waters of the United States in high comfort with very little (and simple) equipment indeed. When contemplating an expensive new chart software package or an anchor that promises superior holding power, remember Hayden and Shackleton and ask: would they want this? Equip your boat with only what you need—what you really need in the true sense of the word. Gadgets are dangerous, because you grow to rely on them. Only your skills as a navigator, sailmaker, carpenter, mechanic, tinkerer, and general jack-of-all-trades are of real importance.

Swallow, our hypothetical little sloop, would be equipped thus:

– Bilge pumps (two manual handy-billies, a rubber bucket, and one electric with float switch)
– Navigation toolkit (covered in Chapter 5)
– Knife, lighter, Chapstick (I always keep these items in my pocket, on land or sea)

Rigging knife

– Binoculars

Marine 7x50 binoculars

– Flashlight (with spare batteries in a waterproof container)
– Lead for sounding with 100 feet of line (Call me old-fashioned, but I've been on countless boats with non-functioning depthsounders.) (covered in Chapter 6)
– First-aid kit
– 4 Fenders

Fenders —

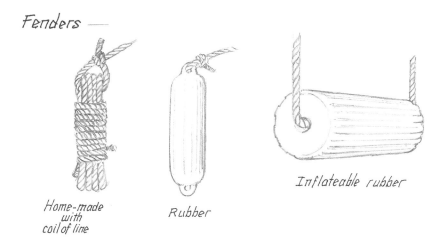

Home-made
with
coil of line

Rubber

Inflateable rubber

- 4 Nylon docking lines, each with an eye splice on one end
- Sound signal (one lung-powered, one air horn)

Lung-powered air horn

- Spare line of various sizes (at least one that is heavy and long enough to be used as a tow rope)
- Spare canvas (for patching sails)
- Sewing kit with leather palm, assorted sailmaker's needles, pliers, Swedish fid, waxed thread, leather scraps (for reinforcing sail corners and for chafing gear), canvas scraps, chunk of beeswax (for helping needle and thread slide through heavy canvas and leather)

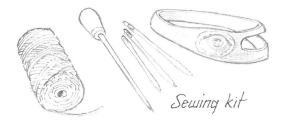

Sewing kit

- Toolbox: handbrace (drill), assorted bits, handsaw, hammer, screwdrivers (Philips and slotted), small assortment of fastenings (nails, screws, shackles, cotter pins); anti-seize lubricant, 3-in-1 oil (not WD-40, which tends to get gummy in the marine environment)—all wrapped in oiled cloth to guard against rust

Useful shipboard tools — to be wrapped in oiled cloth to prevent rust.

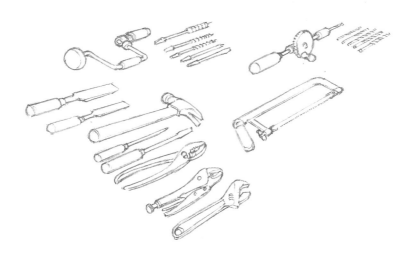

- Engine spares and fluids: Motor oil, coolant, spare zincs, impeller for raw water engine pump
- Fire extinguisher
- Handheld VHF radio
- Hard-wired VHF radio
- Six lifejackets (each with a plastic whistle—won't rust—tied to the collar)
- Flare gun (with spare shells)
- Rope and wood ladder (for climbing aboard)

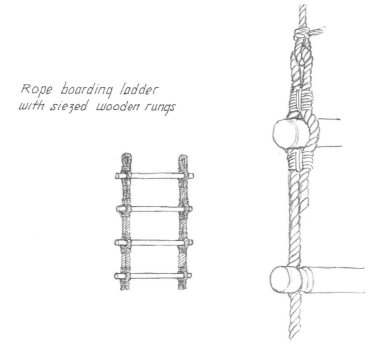

Rope boarding ladder with siezed wooden rungs

– Mask and snorkel (and flippers if you have space)
– Life ring

I mentioned the book *How to Abandon Ship* in the earlier chapter on navigation, but a few more words about it are in order: first, the circumstances of how it came to be written. One of the authors, John J. Banigan, was an officer aboard the first American merchant ship sunk by a Nazi U-boat in May 1941. He and his ten companions survived nineteen days on the high seas, having "encountered mountainous seas, tropical storms, doldrums, and blistering equatorial sun." They effectively sailed away from the sunken vessel and—nearly 900 miles later—were picked up by a Brazilian cargo ship. Each man was healthy and strong; none of the crew was even injured. The book is a tidy summation of seamanship basics, provisioning, and survival skills, all of which are illustrated with hundreds of real-life examples of seamen who were either lost at sea because of a foolish decision or saved because of preparation and presence of mind. It is only 150 pages long, yet "it contains no armchair theory," as it is all taken from actual incidents that occurred during the War.

The point of including it here, however, is to provide yet another glimpse of a perfectly seaworthy vessel, that can handle all the ocean's power, with the simplest and fewest supplies. Example: "WHISTLE—Every man should have a whistle made fast around his neck, so that if he is in the water, he can blow the whistle to draw attention. A severely burned British seaman from a torpedoed gasoline tanker was on the keel of an overturned lifeboat for five days. He was washed off five times, chiefly at night. Since he had a whistle, his shipmates were able to locate him, otherwise he would have been lost."

Mental preparation is as important (or more so) than the gear. Banigan and Richards admonish sailors—it was written with the express purpose of saving lives during the War—to be mentally prepared by frequent drilling, such as launching boats, firing flares, and inspecting gear regularly to be sure it is in its place and in good working condition. Example: "EQUIPMENT – Do not take it for granted that all the equipment required by law is in your lifeboat. Norman Leo Sampson, the third assistant of a torpedoed freighter, reported that nine of his shipmates were trapped in a lifeboat with no oars. The boat drifted into a sea of blazing oil."

Another charm to this often-grisly little book is its succinct writing. I was once at a writer's retreat in which author and *New York Times* columnist Verlyn Klinkenborg used this book as an example of excellent expository writing. You might be reading of people burning to death in a sea of oil or drowning en masse in the suction of a suddenly-sinking ship, but there is no hyperbole. The prose is as neat and vivid as a shot of bourbon.

The chapters "Navigation" and "Open Boat Seamanship" are little gems. At just a handful of pages apiece, the chapters distill the subjects to their essence. Example on seamanship: "*Caution:* When a following sea starts to break on you, do not put the tiller away from the sea. If you do, you will bring the boat broadside toward the oncoming sea—with the danger of being swamped." And an example on navigation: "If your lifeboat is without a navigator, these directions are for you. There is nothing difficult about them. They are simple as directions for a child's game. But they will provide you with the key to your own rescue."

Take the time to understand each piece of equipment, using the gear during moderate and fair conditions or even on shore, if possible. Know which end of you bilge pump to place in the bilge and which end to put over the side (seriously). Practice pumping water from a bucket over the side to be sure the pump's valve isn't stuck or broken. Determine where you will place the pump in the event of a flooding emergency. Can you get the floorboards of the cockpit up? Can you reach the lowest part of the bilge? They say that there is no more efficient bilge pump than a scared man with a bucket, but it's good to practice in a non-emergency.

Think of your boat as an extension of who you are as a person, and equip your boat to reflect this fact. So, if you're more comfortable with mechanical objects, don't frustrate yourself with excessive electronic gear. Similarly, if you're comfortable fiddling around with wires and electronics, a system of powered devices might be more comfortable. However, keep in mind the corrosive nature of the marine environment. The salty, humid air will reduce your coveted items to rust and dust. Most important, keep your boat and its gear within your personal limits. If the limits of the equipment exceed your knowledge or abilities, leave it on the dock or, better yet, on the shelf back in the marine supply store. If the gear is essential, though, at least examine its working parts before you need it.

LIFEJACKETS

The U.S. Coast Guard requires that each boat has a lifejacket for every person on board. In fact, they now require that children under the age of thirteen actually *wear* the lifejacket when they are in small boats. However, many states take this requirement even further.

Life jackets——

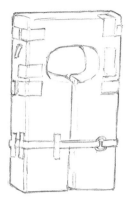

Type I

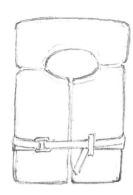

Type II foam

Type III universal fit

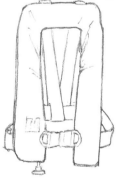

Type II inflateable

Type III inflateable

12 guage safety launcher
with bandolier and four
red aerial signals

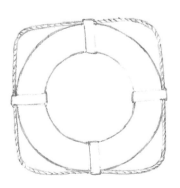

Type IV life ring

It is not uncommon for children under the age of sixteen to be required to wear a life-jacket. Both marine patrol and Coast Guard officers have jurisdiction on this issue and can stop you for a routine safety check to determine the number of lifejackets onboard. Whatever the state or federal law, it's a good idea to wear a lifejacket in a small boat. The Coast Guard reports that 70 percent of boating fatalities are the result of drowning, and 85 percent of these drowning victims are found without a lifejacket on. So it's common sense. And considering how comfortable lifejackets are these days, there's really no excuse. There are just too many ways to get knocked overboard in a small sailboat—not to mention the fact that it could well involve a sharp blow to the head, making the man overboard unconscious before he hits the water. I had a close friend drown this way. He was working on his boat *alongside the dock* when he slipped, fell overboard, and hit his head on the way down. He was working by himself; no one saw him fall. He and I had done several offshore boat deliveries together, neither of us ever imagining that such a fate awaited—the boating equivalent of falling down your back steps and breaking your neck.

Lifejackets are divided into five categories: Type I, II, III, IV, and V. Type I and II lifejackets are the large, horse-collar variety—impossibly uncomfortable to wear around the deck of a boat—but are designed to keep an unconscious victim afloat in an upright position to prevent drowning. These are the kind you see in storage lockers on ferries and other commercial vessels. (Type I are for offshore use; Type II for near shore.)

Type III lifejackets are relatively comfortable to wear and are the kind you see canoeists and Sunfish sailors wearing. They tend to have adjustable straps. They are not designed to right a facedown person into an upright position, however. These are the kind that you want to encourage everyone aboard to wear at all times. And if you intend to invite children aboard, be sure to have child-size lifejackets. Each year the Coast Guard reports numerous children drowned because they slipped out of the adult-sized lifejackets they were wearing. Inflatable lifejackets can be either Type I, II, or III. They allow the wearer to have virtually unlimited range of motion for moving about on board. They are equipped with CO_2 cartridges that inflate air bladders in an instant when a small tablet inside the triggering mechanism is dissolved in water. (Consequently, ensure a dry storage location.) Be aware that these devices have expiration dates and should be inspected regularly. Many inflatable lifejackets are equipped with safety harnesses for buckling into the boat during rough weather.

Type IV lifejackets are throwable devices such as liferings, certain approved buoyant seat cushions, and horseshoes, such as can be used as a lifting sling for a man overboard.

Be aware that Type IV lifejackets (or "PFDs," as the Coast Guard refers to them) are not a replacement for a wearable lifejacket but can only be considered a backup piece of safety equipment.

Type V lifejackets are specialty jackets—such as floating overcoats that are worn by pilots and other commercial mariners. They are intended to be worn at all times and are not considered a replacement for a Type I lifejacket if they are not being worn.

As mentioned in the list of standard equipment aboard *Swallow*, each lifejacket should have a plastic whistle lashed to the collar. While not required, this is a good idea as being lost in the water, once overboard, is a likely scenario. A person afloat in waves is tough to see, especially if there is glare on the water, a choppy sea, or even a moderate swell.

MAN-OVERBOARD PROCEDURE

When a crew member goes over the side unintentionally, the cry of "Man overboard" should be instantaneous. Toss a life ring to the person and head the vessel into the wind so that it comes to a virtual stop. If the boat is moving fast, toss other items into the water, too—anything that will float—so that you make a veritable trail back to him. A boat moving swiftly through the water will leave a drifting victim feeling very alone in the waves in almost no time at all. And once the victim is lost from view, he's nearly as good as lost. The first captain I ever sailed with referred to the ship's taffrail as "the edge of the world."

There's a chilling passage in Richard Henry Dana's *Two Years Before the Mast* that describes this scenario, and its potential result, in vivid detail. A fellow crewmember had fallen from the rig and disappeared immediately in the waves. "We pulled astern, in the direction in which he fell," Dana wrote, "and though we knew there was no hope of saving him, yet no one wished to speak of returning, and we rowed about for nearly an hour, without the hope of doing anything, but unwilling to acknowledge to ourselves that we must give him up."

Assuming you do not lose track of your overboard victim, maneuver the boat in such a way that you can return to the point as quickly as possible—either by backing the sails and allowing the boat to drift down to the person in the water or by dropping sails and motoring or rowing to him.

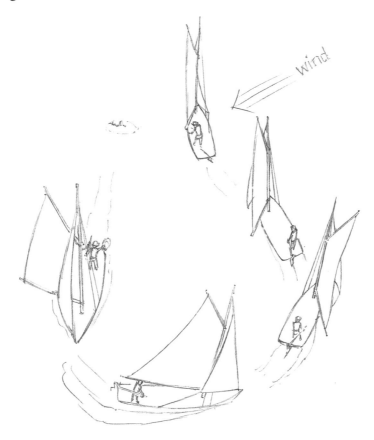

Pick up of an overboard victim from an upwind hove-to position.

You should position the boat broadside to the person in the water with the vessel upwind. This forms a small slick on the sea surface that will shelter the victim from breaking waves. And the force of the wind will keep the boat drifting sideways toward him. How to retrieve the victim depends on a few factors: whether he is conscious, the size of the boat and its "freeboard" (height of the deck above the sea), and how many of you are left on board to effect a rescue. Recovering an unconscious victim from the water shorthandedly can be done, but it requires great seamanship. If the sails are still up, the jib should be positioned aback and the helm hard over. This is a classic "hove-to" position (more on this in Chapter 2)—the jib pushing the bow downwind and the tiller attempting to push the bow in the opposite direction. This results in a sideways-crabbing motion that essentially stops the vessel in the water with the wind just off the bow. You can ride out a storm hove to; you can pick up a man overboard; you can have your lunch and a peaceful cup of tea. It's a way to rest without dropping sail.

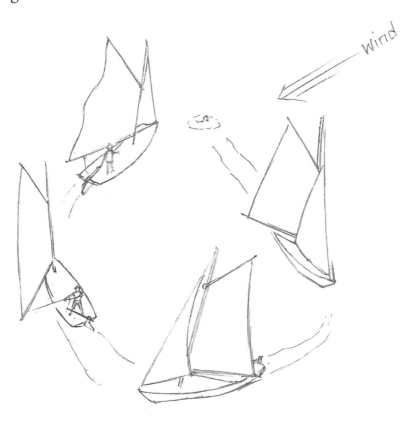

Gybe-pick up of an overboard victim from the leeward side.

In *The Compleat Cruiser*, Herreshoff suggests *gybing* following a man-overboard incident. This maneuver allows the boat to approach the victim to leeward of the previous course. In this way, "the boat or yacht would come to a standstill just as she was abreast the [victim]." This sounds a little tricky, but it might be worth experimenting with in fair weather, especially since there is not a perfect man-overboard response maneuver that can be effective in all conditions.

Once the boat is positioned alongside the victim, you can either drag him aboard bodily—not an easy task with a limp adult in wet clothing—or rig a sling that is attached to a halyard for mechanical advantage. *Swallow* is likely too small a boat to winch someone aboard in this way, but the sides are also not so high as to make recovering an overboard victim such a challenge either.

If the victim is conscious, you simply have to position the boat as above and have them climb over the lee rail and roll—ignominiously but alive—onto the deck. You can also rig a rope and wood ladder (which is great for swimming over the side, too), tied to the rail or lashed to a cleat. A metal ladder works just as well and is a little easier to climb.

GOING OVER THE SIDE

No ladder?

A spare line looped over the side with ends tied widely apart along the gunwale is a useful substitute if tied high enough for the swimmer to get a leg over the side.

There will be times when you will need to consider going into the water, whether for maintenance, checking the condition of equipment below the waterline, or diving on an anchor or mooring to check how well it is set. First, consider the temperature. Even relatively warm water can be dangerous if you need to spend more than a minute underwater. In the so-called temperate regions, the frigid waters will cause hypothermia in just a few minutes. Consider purchasing a wetsuit; even a "shorty" will offer some protection from the chill.

Sailing in Maine aboard a boat with an inboard engine I usually carry a full wetsuit: gloves, hood, booties, and full-size suit. Snagging a lobster buoy in your propeller can take a few minutes to disentangle; doing so without a suit, which I have done many times, leaves me blue-lipped and shaking. A wetsuit also offers abrasion protection. Working under a rolling hull is dirty work. Barnacles will cut skin to ribbons, a propeller blade can inflict a nasty cut, and getting slightly bumped on the head can knock you senseless. A hood acts like a helmet, and neoprene gloves protect your hands—all while keeping you warm!

I also always carry a mask and snorkel so that I can visually inspect the outside of the hull or propulsion system. You can clear a tangled prop in a minute if you can see well and are protected from the cold. A serrated knife works best cutting kelp, fishing nets, or "pot warp" free, especially if the line is polypropylene, which tends to "weld" itself around the shaft because of the heat. Be exceedingly careful clearing a propeller with a folding knife. It will almost assuredly close on your fingers. A fixed blade is essential.

Wearing the above gear is also convenient for scrubbing the algae off the bottom of the boat. In areas of heavy marine growth, you will find that your boat accumulates a green beard or long tags or clumps of mussels. Go over the side carrying a scrub brush and work your way around the hull. To combat heavy growth you may need a putty knife—just be careful not to scratch the hull.

Whenever you go over the side, be sure to have another crew member on deck be your buddy. That person will watch for your safety and can also serve as a gofer—to retrieve additional tools or to be an extra pair of hands. It may also be helpful to rig a few lines under the hull, passing from one rail, beneath the keel, to the other rail. This is a good way to move around the slippery exterior of the hull.

Equipping a boat for daysailing can be done inexpensively and with little effort. Once you have the objects, though, they need a home onboard. If each object has its place, where it is returned after each use, the boat will be a much safer and pleasurable craft to sail.

8

BOAT MAINTENANCE

"Six days shalt thou labor and do all that thou art able, and on the seventh— holystone the decks and scrape the cable."

—from *Two Years Before the Mast*, by Richard Henry Dana

My friend Sam Manning, co-venturer in this book, once caught me engaged in what he considered a vile act. I was clutching a powerful orbital sander and sanding the cabin top of an old schooner, preparing her for the season during the annual spring "fit-out." Dust was swirling about me like a Saharan sandstorm. I was wearing a dust mask over my mouth and nose; my body and clothing were covered in a fine, white powder. He came up to me on the dock and must have been watching me for a while before I noticed him standing there.

"Do you *enjoy* doing that?" he asked when I had shut the machine down and pulled the dust mask up on my forehead so I could chat.

I looked at my clothes; I could only imagine what my face looked like with paint dust worked into every crease. "Well, uh…not really," I said.

"Then why do it?"

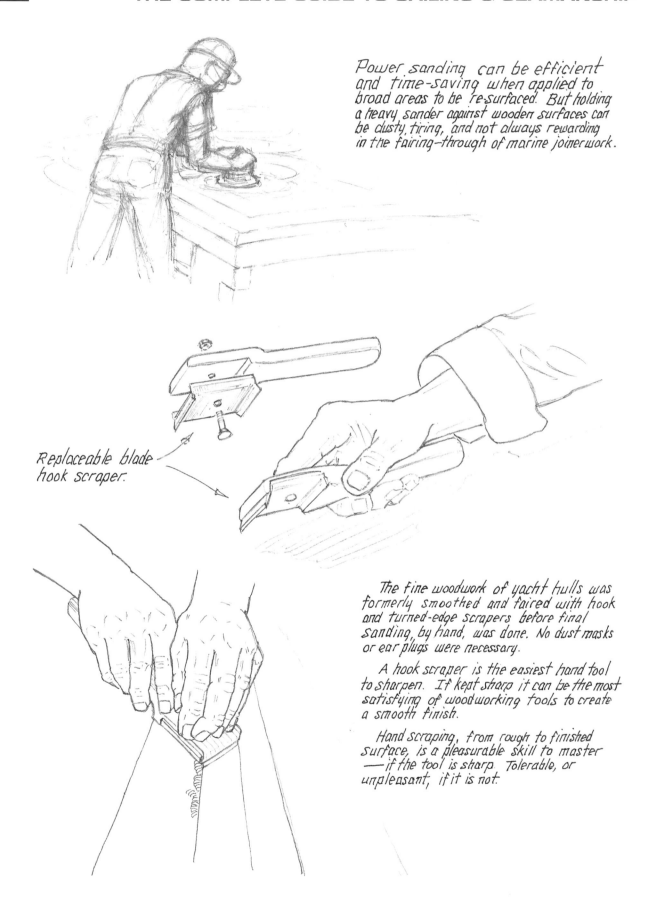

Power sanding can be efficient and time-saving when applied to broad areas to be re-surfaced. But holding a heavy sander against wooden surfaces can be dusty, tiring, and not always rewarding in the fairing-through of marine joinerwork.

Replaceable blade hook scraper.

The fine woodwork of yacht hulls was formerly smoothed and faired with hook and turned-edge scrapers before final sanding, by hand, was done. No dust masks or ear plugs were necessary.

A hook scraper is the easiest hand tool to sharpen. If kept sharp it can be the most satisfying of woodworking tools to create a smooth finish.

Hand scraping, from rough to finished surface, is a pleasurable skill to master —if the tool is sharp. Tolerable, or unpleasant, if it is not.

At first I wondered what he meant. Why sand a boat? So you can paint it afterward. It's what one did in spring. But then it occurred to me, knowing Sam to be a traditionalist, that he must have been referring to the electric sander in my hand. "Do I have a choice?" I ventured.

And that was the moment he was waiting for. He climbed aboard and grabbed a paint scraper, felt the edge of the blade and, running his thumb along it, made a show of indicating its dullness. "Do you have a mill file?" he asked. I thought I had, so I rummaged in a tool box and soon handed one over. He took the file, held the scraper firmly on its side so that it was overhanging the edge of the cabin top, and began pressing the file onto the blade, drawing it across the beveled edge in slow but skilled motions. He did it ten or twelve times and then instructed me to do the same. I was clumsy at first, the file skidding with a hideous screech of metal on metal until I found the groove and was able to feel the keening of the blade.

Sam then took the scraper back and in a few quick swipes had peeled back a section of old paint, exposing the wood, and in a few more swipes had feathered the cracked paint beautifully. He quickly covered a large section of the cabin trunk. It might have taken me twice as long on the sander, and I may not have discovered the loose spots in the paint that the pressure of the scraper had uncovered.

"A skilled man with a sharp scraper can do more than any fool with a sander," he said. "You can choose to surround yourself with dust and noise or you can gain skill with one of these. See you tomorrow!" He grinned at me, handed the scraper back, and stepped off the boat. He and his wife, Susan, were soon rowing away in their Banks dory on their daily row out Camden Harbor—around Curtis Island and the seabuoy and back, leaving me to contemplate the Zen of paint scrapers and the lack of it in a hateful orbital sander. Sam and Susan do this just about every day of the year and have done for decades, regardless of weather. Over the course of two years I lived in Camden (and for more than fifteen years of correspondence), I came to know about wooden boat maintenance and some of the old ways of seamanship that Sam and Susan have gleaned from decades of experience.

The point Sam made to me that day was how to use a pair of simple tools—a paint scraper and a metal file. But the more salient point I took away from that brief encounter is that the act of working on a boat should be every bit as enjoyable as sailing the boat. From that moment on I've preferred wooden boats. I would much rather be surrounded by sawdust and paint flakes than gelcoat, epoxy resin, and micro-shards of glass fiber.

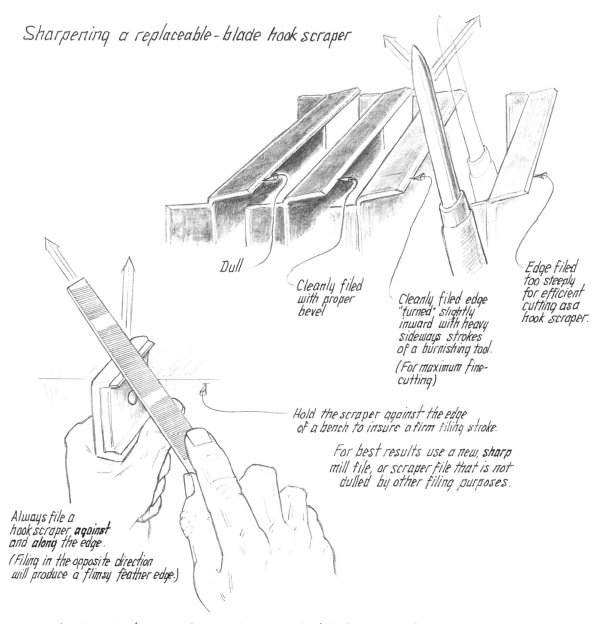

Sharpening a replaceable-blade hook scraper

Dull

Cleanly filed
with proper
bevel

Cleanly filed edge
"turned" slightly
inward with heavy
sideways strokes
of a burnishing tool.
(For maximum fine-
cutting)

Edge filed
too steeply
for efficient
cutting as a
hook scraper.

Hold the scraper against the edge
of a bench to insure a firm filing stroke.

For best results use a new, sharp
mill file, or scraper file that is not
dulled by other filing purposes.

Always file a
hook scraper **against**
and **along** the edge.
(Filing in the opposite direction
will produce a flimsy feather edge.)

This four-eared replaceable-blade model seems to have the best steel and the most reserve of the various hook scrapers
offered in stores today. As you become skillful with this tool, you'll gladly file an ear or two away in the course
of a project while enjoying the finished work of a really sharp scraper.

Wooden boats require their share of noxious chemicals, to be fair, but, on average, far
less than fiberglass ones. They also allow for the use of simple tools rather than a reliance
on fussing with chemical compounds. The other reason I enjoy wooden boats is that
I have the skills to work on them. A wooden boat is simply a large, interlocking puzzle.
When one piece fails, you cut it out and replace it with one of the same shape. Sure, there

are complex angles and tricky techniques to accomplish these tasks, but it's all a matter of degree. The idea is the same whether you're replacing a section of cap rail, a new plank, or an entire stem. Take out the rotten bits and put in strong, new ones.

Okay, enough sanctimony. The owner of a fiberglass boat would counter that the complete *lack* of annual maintenance is the reason to own fiberglass. You might only have to apply gelcoat once over a lifetime of ownership if you're not fussy about that showboat gleam. While I'm replacing rotten bits and putting in new ones, he or she's out sailing on the bay and has been since the first hint of fine weather.

There is a fine section on boat repair and maintenance in Herreshoff's *Compleat Cruiser* entitled "Goddard's Workshop." Goddard is showing his friend Coridon around his workshop, a twenty-five by twelve-and-one-half-foot space equipped with a fireplace, wash sink, north-facing windows, banks of drawers for tools, and only two power tools in the whole place—an electric drill and a lathe. "Most of the power tools make a lot of dust and dirt, and they often take more time to set up or adjust and sharpen than the whole job would take with a hand tool," Goddard says. "You will say, young man, 'How about the work?' and I will answer you that the exercise of using most of the hand tools is very beneficial, particularly light planing and sawing, so by the use of hand tools one can combine healthy exercise with pleasure, and at the same time be producing something that is useful and attractive."

One other clever feature to Goddard's woodshop was a pair of comfortable chairs positioned to maximize southern exposure. Since sailors invariably know everything and want to dispense advice, you have to incorporate this fact seamlessly into any shop's design. Goddard explained: "When you are building a boat of any kind there will always be one or two of the neighbors who will want to tell you how to do it, and I find if there are a couple of comfortable chairs out of the way it is much better to have them smoke themselves into semi-consciousness than have them in the way, leaning up against the work bench."

Goddard found that by giving windbags a comfortable, out-of-the-way perch, he could safely ignore them in a friendly way. "I have trained myself to entirely disregard their conversation and they do not bother me at all," he continued. "I simply say, 'Yes,' 'Is that so?' or 'You don't say so!' In this way, they have the satisfaction of being great oracles while all the time I am quite undisturbed.

Whatever your choice of hull material, the point of this chapter is to treat your boat—its hull, its systems, and its rig—with genuine care. Herreshoff's Goddard would even add one's tools to the list of items requiring care. He went so far as to advocate washing one's hands prior to handling tools to prevent them from rusting. Following are a series of basic maintenance activities that will prolong the life of your boat, keep you safe in the process of sailing your boat, and offer years of enjoyment along the way.

ENGINE CLEANING

Swallow has an inboard engine, a 15-hp diesel. (I would like to think that in the hypothetical boat that we've created I have also created a beautifully *clean* engine.) If your engine is clean, *really* clean, then you are on the way to being a good boat owner. This is because cleaning an engine takes time. Oil spills and then hardens onto the engine block when it gets hot. It leaks down between hoses, covering hose clamps and hiding potential problems. Oil leaks into the bilge and pretty soon the inside of your boat is a slimy mess. By taking the time to wipe the engine clean, you're spending time with your engine; you're engaged in a relationship with it, instead of seeing it as a mystical piece of equipment that is removed from the true enjoyment of your boat—using the sails. So, if you choose to have an engine, whether an outboard or an inboard, take the time to wipe it down frequently. This is where engine maintenance starts.

It may be helpful to channel the protagonist in *Zen and the Art of Motorcycle Maintenance*, the fictional Phaedrus who insisted on checking his motorcycle's timing frequently as he climbed altitude in the Rockies. He checked air pressure, fiddled with the carburetor's fuel-air mixture, and performed his own oil and filter changes on the side of the road or in campgrounds. He carried a small packet of tools and spares in his saddle bags. His companion, whose relationship with his motorcycle was less engaged— he turned the key and expected it to not only start but run flawlessly since he'd paid someone to maintain the machine—would also be the kind of person to expect his boatyard crew to maintain his engine, tune the rig, and get everything shipshape prior to his day of sailing. This is all fine so long as things go according to plan. But it does not produce a self-reliant sailor.

When you refill the fluids (oil, antifreeze, and fuel) be sure to put absorbent pads beneath the spouts and wipe any excess off immediately. A note of caution: oily rags have the potential to burst into flame spontaneously! Do not throw them in a rubbish bin belowdecks. Air them out on deck until they are truly dry or dispose of them in a proper shoreside facility for this purpose.

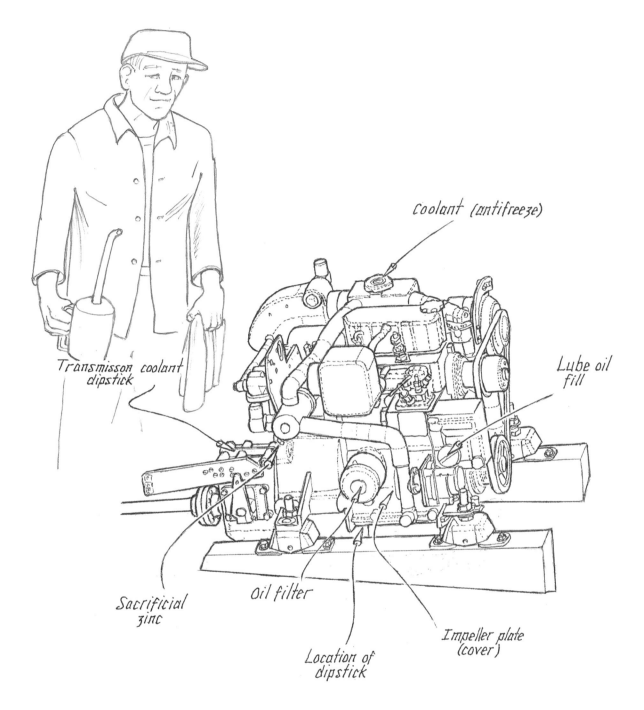

Coolant (antifreeze)

Lube oil fill

Transmisson coolant dipstick

Sacrificial zinc

Oil filter

Location of dipstick

Impeller plate (cover)

Check the oil level daily by pulling the dipstick, wiping it clean with a rag or paper towel, and then reinserting the stick and pulling it out again to read the level and inspect the quality of the oil. You should also check on the engine manufacturer's recommended oil change schedule. Frequent startings might require the engine oil to be changed every 100 hours, whereas an engine that runs for long periods of time may only require an oil change every 200 hours. This is because the hardest thing on a diesel engine is frequent ignitions followed by short run times. Every time you start the engine, the pistons slide in their cylinders, metal on metal, without full lubrication until they've been running for a few minutes. This is because the oil drains down into the pan after the engine is secured. However, running the engine for long periods of time is what a diesel is built for. It is far better to run a diesel engine for ten hours straight than it is to turn it on and off ten times in one day. As much as it may pain a sailor to do so, each starting should be followed by at least twenty minutes of engine operation. This allows the engine to become fully lubricated and allows any condensation in the fuel to be burned and filtered out.

Even if you don't reach the number of hours recommended between oil changes in one season, you should change the lubricating oil every season. Do so by first running the engine for twenty minutes—the heat brings out the impurities of the oil pan and suspended in the oil itself—and then, when it's good and hot, pump out the old crankcase oil. Be sure to change the filter during each oil change, first smearing the gasket with fresh oil to create a tight seal. Lastly, once you've changed the engine oil, be sure to run the engine on its fresh oil. This circulates the fresh oil into the seals and cylinders and ensures a clean start to your next season. Changing lubricating oil is a messy job, and you will inevitably burn your hands in hot oil and spill some in the bilge. But you'll feel like you're giving your investment the care it deserves and also have a sense of satisfaction that comes with interacting with your machine. In his 2010 polemic *Shop Class as Soulcraft*, author Matthew Crawford posits that working on machines, in ways large and small, offers a sense of "individual agency" that is increasingly nonexistent in a culture that encourages helplessness. He cites the lack of oil dipsticks in recent Mercedes Benz models (a computer must check the oil level) as a particularly appalling example. As consumers we've become so dependent on disposable modern contrivances that we lack manual competence to the point that our hands are becoming increasingly like foreign objects. He speaks of the "ethics of maintenance and repair"—whether of our washers and dryers, our automobiles and motorcycles, or our various other machines—the pursuit of which ultimately nourishes individual agency and self-reliance. Or, as he puts it another way, "real knowledge arises through confrontations with real things." Who knew that changing one's oil could be so philosophical!

BILGE CHECKS

The bilge is another area you should learn to know intimately. There is not a single place on your boat that you should not be able to comfortably place your hands for an inspection. Floorboards should come up easily to allow a full inspection of the bilge area. Do not allow any standing water anywhere in your boat, regardless of hull material. Even a fiberglass boat will, over time, absorb moisture into the core, requiring expensive repairs. Keep bilges dry, sponging out the areas that are not accessible by bilge pumps.

SCRAPING AND PAINTING

There's not much to say about scraping and painting a fiberglass boat, with the exception of the annual cleaning and painting of anti-fouling paint on the bottom of the hull. This is best accomplished with a pressure-washer, but a scrub brush and garden hose will serve equally well if you don't mind getting a little dirty. Most marine life comes right off, especially if it's been sitting out of the water all winter. Bottom paints have become less noxious than in decades past, but they still contain enough harmful chemicals to be known to the State of California to cause cancer, as just about every marine product on the market today does. So you don't want these paint flakes mixing with your lawn or garden beds. The best method would be to catch as much of the flaking mess in a drop cloth spread beneath the boat, and then toss the flakes into a plastic bag for disposal in the hazardous-waste section of your local transfer station. Of course, no boatyard in the world does this (with a few exceptions), but that doesn't mean the chemicals are safe to mingle in your groundwater. Two other warnings about applying bottom paint: (1) stir the heck out of a can before applying it (at least twenty to thirty minutes), since the solids settle on the bottom, and, (2) apply the paint on launch day. Bottom paint works best when it's still wet when the boat goes in the water. Once your boat is afloat, you will need to scrub growth from the waterline regularly, anywhere from every few weeks to only once or twice a season, depending on your climate and your level of fastidiousness.

Much can be said about scraping and painting a wooden boat, however. And plenty of books are devoted to this very subject such that it doesn't make sense to repeat it all here, except to provide a few annual maintenance suggestions. First, storing a wooden boat in winter is best done on a dirt floor. This is because it will continue to be subjected to moisture that comes up from the earth. (A concrete floor will dry out a hull.) And a loosely fitting canvas, wood, or metal cover—something that allows for the free passage of air—is best for the deck and topsides. Skrink-wrapping a boat, any boat, in fact, is deadly. It traps moisture. If you do shrink-wrap your boat, be careful to provide for the passage of air underneath, both fore and aft and athwartships.

Winter Cover ——

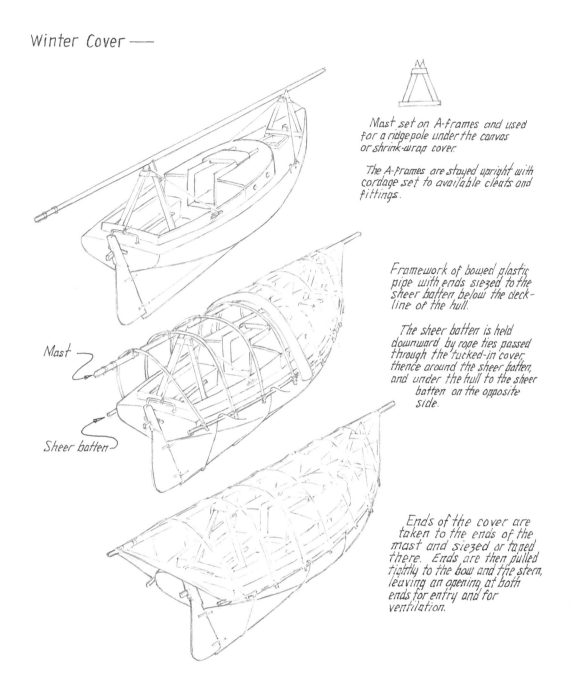

Mast set on A-frames and used for a ridgepole under the canvas or shrink-wrap cover.

The A-frames are stayed upright with cordage set to available cleats and fittings.

Framework of bowed plastic pipe with ends siezed to the sheer batten below the deck-line of the hull.

The sheer batten is held downward by rope ties passed through the tucked-in cover, thence around the sheer batten, and under the hull to the sheer batten on the opposite side.

Mast

Sheer batten

Ends of the cover are taken to the ends of the mast and siezed or taped there. Ends are then pulled tightly to the bow and the stern, leaving an opening at both ends for entry and for ventilation.

In spring, you'll need to scrape the loose paint, prime the bare wood *on the same day as it is scraped,* and then fill the seams between planks with seam compound. Only then is a wooden hull ready to receive paint. And even then, it will leak when it is launched. This can be a harrowing experience to the uninitiated—watching water pour into the bilges of your freshly-painted boat. But it's what wood boats do. If you've done your job reasonably well, the seams will take up and she'll stop leaking in a day or so. If not, you may have sprung some caulking (or have larger problems, but that's for another day). Another benefit to a wooden boat that takes in a little water is the reminder that a boat needs attention. You simply can't put it out on the mooring for the season, regardless of hull type, and expect it to remain afloat. One way or another, if you don't pay regular attention, it will fill with water and sink, either because the electric bilge pump will clog, or because it ran out of battery power, or because some mysterious set of circumstances have simply conspired against you. So a little water in the bilges is nature's way of reminding you that your boat needs you!

LUBRICATING HARDWARE: SEACOCKS, PUMPS, & HINGES

Any piece of hardware with moving parts needs maintenance. Shackles should never be secured without a liberal dousing of anti-seize lubricant (usually a graphite paste) around the threads. You simply will not get them undone at the end of the season if you have not done so. Seacocks—the valves that are the through-hull fittings for hoses—require annual cleaning and lubrication with a heavy waterproof grease. Disassemble the valve once the boat is out of the water and smear the grease on the threads and the ball-and-socket (or in the gate, if that's the style), being sure to work the grease well inside. Hinges need regular oil, and pumps should be inspected for damaged or cracked flaps and impellers with missing blades. Whatever your hardware list is, get on a schedule and stick with it. Both your spring fit-out and winterization procedures should include a checklist that is followed every year.

RIG INSPECTION

There is a well-known adage about the level of trust you should place in your boatyard's rigger. Since the rigger will be home safely in his bed when your rigging failure occurs, you should, as Ronald Reagan once quipped, "Trust but verify." Inspect that your stays and shrouds have been not just tightly secured but the shackles and turnbuckles also "moused" with wire (wrapping wire through the eye of the shackle pin and back through the U of the shackle, so that the pin cannot work loose). Be satisfied with your tension, and ask questions of your rigger (if you have one) regarding the appropriate tension. Consider a replacement schedule for your wire stays so that you're not simply replacing them as they break. Metal fatigue is the most common reason for rigging failure—and it is almost always sudden and unpleasant. Rigging manufacturers have standards for these, but they do no good unless they are heeded by the boat owner.

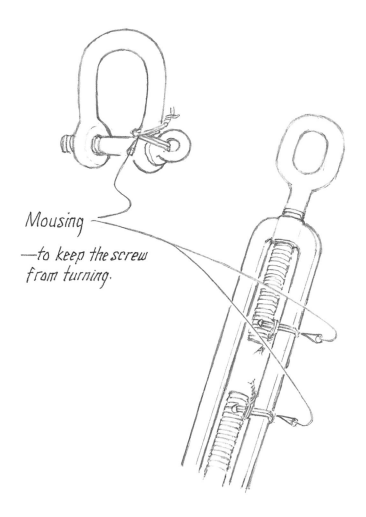

Mousing
—to keep the screw
from turning.

SAIL CARE

Sails deteriorate in UV light and saltwater, and they wear out because of the friction involved in raising and lowering sails, chafing against the rig, and repeated folding and furlings. You want your sails to wear out; it means you're using them. But you want them to wear out on schedule, not prematurely. So, folding sails (as opposed to stuffing them) extends their life, as does covering them from the sun and not putting them away wet. While most sails won't rot anymore, they will certainly mildew and take on a horrible smell, not to mention ugly stains.

SALTWATER WASH OF HULL

Wooden boats like saltwater. Rain is bad, and standing rainwater puddles are worse, but a good saltwater bath for a wooden boat is like a pickling—a great way to ward off rot and keep the seams tight. This is counterintuitive to fiberglass boatowners, who bathe their boats in freshwater at marinas after a day's sail.

WINTERIZING YOUR ENGINE

Getting your boat ready for winter requires a few basic procedures to ward against freezing temperatures and the corrosive effects of sitting fuel. First, dump a measured amount of biocide (or fuel stabilizer for gas engines) into your tank. You'll want to leave your tank relatively full in winter, since this lessens the volume of air and therefore condensation that will accumulate in your tanks over the winter. Algae forms in the condensation and then mixes with the fuel. Once you have poured the correct volume of stabilizer into your tank, be sure to run the engine long enough that you are confident that you have run the stabilizer through the engine's fuel system as well. Whether you change your fuel filters (primary and secondary) at the start of your season or at the end is up to you, but you should pick one method and stick with it.

Next, remove your raw water intake hose from inside the vessel (once the boat is hauled out!). Then, dump several gallons of nontoxic antifreeze into a five-gallon bucket. Start your engine and hold the intake hose in the pail until you are confident that all the seawater has been pumped through the engine. You may need someone to pour antifreeze into the bucket to keep up with the pump and someone else outside the vessel hollering when he sees antifreeze coming out the wet exhaust. The point is to flush all the seawater from the engine. (If you have a freshwater system in your boat for sinks or heads, you'll likely want to perform this task using cheap vodka instead of antifreeze, since you won't have traces of antifreeze in your potable water system come spring, and vodka leaves no aftertaste, so to speak.)

Next, remove your raw water impeller and tie it to the engine so you don't forget all about it in the spring. Some people replace their impeller at the start of each season, but as long as it remains flexible and the rubber blades intact, there's no need to do so that frequently. The important thing is not to forget to reinstall it when you go to restart the engine.

Change the engine's sacrificial zinc. This is something you should be in the habit of doing throughout the season anyway, but it's a good idea to put a fresh one in at the end of the season. Each harbor has its own level of electricity traveling through the water (silently corroding your engine's metals), so there is no rule of thumb as to how often a zinc should be changed. Don't wait until your engine's zinc is completely deteriorated before changing it. If it is virtually gone and crumbling away to nothing when you touch it, you've waited too long.

BATTERIES

If your boat has one or two batteries for starting the engine and running a small bank of cabin lights, winterize your batteries simply by disconnecting them and bringing them home to your basement or some other non-freezing location. Fill the cells with distilled water and then bring them up to a full charge about once a month through the winter.

A busy family needs a simple boat.

In the end, the required maintenance of a sailboat should inform the kind of boat you choose to own. For a while, when my children were very young, I could only manage a sixteen-foot, ABS-plastic canoe. Now, with four children between the ages of eight and sixteen, I believe I'm ready for a fourteen-foot, wooden Banks dory with a small sailing rig. It needs a new sheer plank and a total overhaul of its seams, but I believe I'm ready for the challenge. And while larger boats call to me, I know my limits from past experience owning and operating a variety of wooden and steel boats. Maybe, by the time I'm retired, I'll be ready again for a boat the size and complexity of *Swallow*. While this is an exaggeration, the point here is to strive for a sense of confidence in your maintenance schedule, a confidence that only comes with knowing that you are thoroughly prepared for the vicissitudes of wind and waves.

9

DAILY RHYTHMS: A DAY ON THE WATER

"Jukes remained indifferent, as if rendered irresponsible by the force of the hurricane, which made the very thought of action utterly vain."

—from *Typhoon,* by Joseph Conrad

I rose early, just as dawn was breaking, and walked down to the beach. In the blue-gray light I could just make out the surface of the sea—dotted with whitecaps. The wind was blowing onshore—southwest—as it had been all night and was still fresh. I had read the report the night before that the breeze, fifteen to twenty knots from the northwest, should last until midday and then it would diminish to ten to fifteen knots in the afternoon. It sounded like a perfect day, actually, but would involve an exciting start. My daughter Raven and I had been planning our sail for over a week—watching the weather as the day approached, hoping we could reach Inner Green Island for a picnic lunch and afternoon swim. We would bring our snorkels, since I had heard of a wreck that lay in shallow water on the far side of the island. We would have no trouble reaching the island in this breeze. We would anchor in a sheltered cove on the northeast side of the island.

I returned home and, as the coffee brewed, turned on the computer to recheck the weather forecast. It was unchanged, but I made a note in my notebook under the date (*NW 15 to 20 kts morning, 10 to 15 in afternoon*) along with a note on the tide (*Lo 10:46am; Hi 5:07pm*). There was no fog predicted for the day, which was a relief. In a few minutes, Raven had heard my rustling and came crashing down the stairs. Despite my admonishments not to wake her brothers, she was too delighted with our plans to contain her energy. I shared the weather report with her, and we ate a quiet breakfast as the first rays of the sun began to shine in the kitchen window. We made sandwiches, packed some fruit, and topped off our water jug. Raven grabbed the oars and lifejackets from the shed, and, after putting our lifejackets on, we started down to the beach. The dinghy was upside down on the beach, its painter tied in a bowline around a tree. I untied the line, flipped it over, and then together we carried it down the beach, placing it at the water's edge. Kicking off my shoes, I dragged the boat into the shallows so it wouldn't slam in the surf, and held it steady as Raven loaded the gear into the bow. She clambered in, grabbed the oars, and I turned the boat so its nose was pointed seaward. With a final push off the beach, I climbed over the transom and plunked myself down in the stern. Raven took short, quick strokes, and we were soon in deep water, bobbing over the waves like a duck.

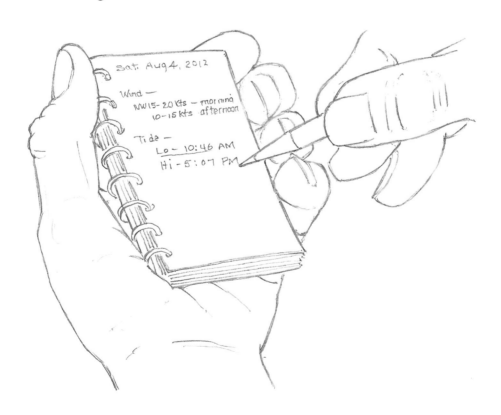

My vintage *American Merchant Seaman's Manual* has an entire chapter devoted to rowing. Entitled, "Handling Small Boats Under Oars," the chapter opens with a short list on the primary purposes of rowboats for sea service: "1. to weather any storm; 2. to be rowed some distance when necessary; and 3. to land on a beach where the surf is heavy."

This is actually pretty good advice for a dinghy that serves a small sailboat or yacht. While a dinghy is not a lifeboat, per se, it should certainly be a seaworthy craft that can carry people and a small load of gear. Consider Quoyle, the antihero in Annie Proulx's *The Shipping News*. The crude skiff he bought had such a low transom that a stern wave mounted from behind when he backed off on the outboard's throttle swamped the boat. "Look at it," said his friend Dennis. "It's just a few planks bunged together. The boy that built it deserves a whack of shot in the backside."

A dinghy should also row well, by tracking in a straight line so that it is not too tiring or frustrating to row it some distance. There may be times when your mooring or anchorage is far from the beach or dock. This little dinghy should be one you're comfortable with and enjoy rowing. Lastly, it should be able to be beached in reasonably rough surf. A slender dinghy with lovely lines might be completely impractical for landing in surf if it has low freeboard, because, like Quoyle's, it will be instantly swamped.

Rowing well is a great skill and is not to be underestimated. I had a sailing friend who was fond of saying that a twelve-foot dinghy can make an ass out of the most experienced captain. It's worth putting the time into managing a boat under oars. One way to do that is to row away from a dock and back again—again and again until you can do it gracefully. To land a dinghy alongside a dock or another vessel, approach at a 45-degree angle and then, at the last minute, ship the oar and oarlock on the side of the dock or other vessel, and then, just as it appears that the dinghy will strike, place the outer oar into the water and hold water. This forces the stern into the dock and places the dinghy neatly alongside. Without changing your seating position, you should be able to reach out your hand and place it gently on the dock to fend off.

And this is exactly what Raven did, pulling alongside *Swallow* as though the oars were extensions of her arms and the boat attuned with her wishes. She grabbed the rail to steady us, and I climbed aboard, gathered the gear from the dinghy's bow, and grabbed hold of the painter. Raven climbed aboard herself.

I lashed the painter to a cleat, choosing to keep the dinghy alongside until the engine was started and we were underway. This would keep the skiff's painter from fouling in the propeller and keep it from bumping annoyingly beneath the overhang of the stern.

We stowed our lunch in the little cabin, removed the sail covers, and pulled out the chart to go over our plans. Inner Green Island lay some five miles to the east as the crow flies. We traced our route and imagined the direction of the wind in relation to it. We would sail on a beam reach to the north end of our island and then nose out into Hussey Sound on a broad reach. There might be a swell in the Hussey, which might make for lumpy conditions, but the strong breeze would keep us moving and not cause us to wallow uncomfortably in the swell. We remembered that the tide would be low just before 11:00 AM, meaning we'd be riding out the last of the ebb current in the Sound and then likely be at our destination at just about low water. We would then ride the tide back home again—downhill both ways!—sailing on a close reach.

In *Oceanography and Seamanship*, William van Dorn considers the following statistic: the U.S. Coast Guard spends 80 percent of its time rendering assistance to private yachts; 19 percent of its time for small documented and commercial vessels (typically fishing vessels and other small workboats), and the remaining 1 percent for large commercial vessels. He compares this figure to the long tradition dating from the earliest seafaring times until the early 20th century—a time of "wooden ships and iron men"—when "every seaman knew how to hand, reef, and steer." The majority of these incidents requiring

rescue, he writes, are the result of poor seamanship, failure to keep a proper lookout, for example, or bungling the simplest of seamanship tasks.

While technology has advanced such that ships and yachts are technically safer than ever before in history, the practical skills of sailors have deteriorated to the point of helplessness. "Ships and yachts are now larger, stronger, and faster, but there seems to be room for improved seamanship," he wrote.

But what is seamanship? Where does it begin? Can there be a checklist of skills that combine to create a catalog of seamanship? Certainly, I've always felt that good seamanship is about the littlest things, basic skills and simple habits, which is what this book is a collection of: how well a line is coiled, whether the ends of the lines on a boat are properly whipped or simply wrapped in tape. Handling a dinghy is as important as navigating; paying attention to the weather is as vital as keeping your bilge pump in good working order. But seamanship is more than just a laundry list of skills and habits. It would seem that by accumulating enough skills and good habits, you also begin to develop judgment, and that is the essence of good seamanship: knowing when a set of skills and habits come to bear in a given set of circumstances so as to lead to a decisive choice about a course of action. In our little excursion to Inner Green Island on the Maine coast, Raven and I had talked about the destination, paid attention to the weather in the days leading up to our trip, even talked about the possibility of either changing our destination or postponing the trip altogether if the weather was unfavorable. (I've gotten into the worst trouble at sea because of tight, inflexible schedules.) She had the skills to handle the dinghy because of previous experience. She knew how to read a chart in an elemental way. We discussed the route in context with the day's forecast. We'd gotten enough sleep the night before. We dressed for the weather. We respected and *liked* each other's company.

When French sailor Bernard Moitessier sailed into Cape Town Bay on March 18, 1969, he scribbled a message on a scrap of paper, stuffed it into a film canister, and then shot it aboard the deck of a British tanker using a slingshot. A surprised British officer retrieved the canister and read the following message: "I am continuing non-stop toward the Pacific Islands because I am happy at sea, and perhaps also to save my soul."

Moitessier was engaged in the Golden Globe, the first nonstop round-the-world yacht race, and he was stomping up the final sea miles in anticipation of winning the race and its prize money when he had a sudden change of heart. He had no radio transmitter aboard his ketch *Joshua*, so he relied on Stone Age communication to convey his simple message. He had no interest in the adulation of the crowds, the prize money, and the inevitable fame that would come from being the first person to sail alone—nonstop—around the world. He would keep going, sailing off to the South Pacific for a few more months of peace. And this is what he did.

How is this story applicable here? Because it conveys hints of the essence of good seamanship. He had such confidence in his skills and his judgment, and was enjoying himself so profusely, that continuing alone, halfway 'round the world after having sailed completely around the world, that he would keep sailing simply for the love of it—for the joy of his adventure rather than the acclaim.

"*Joshua* has taken me beyond my dreams, where time ceased to exist," Moitessier wrote. Or, in the words of his biographer Jean-Michel Barrault, "The lone sailor had achieved perfect freedom. He was in perfect harmony with the sea, the sky, and the wind."

You hear often of this *oneness* in sea literature. American poet Gary Snyder wrote of it during his time spent on oil tankers, of all things ("the ship burns with a furnace heart / steam veins and copper nerves"). And in fiction, Jan de Hartog referred to it repeatedly in his *Captain* trilogy ("the sounds of the ship were all around me…I felt as if I were a part of her, as if we formed one body, of which I was the center of awareness; all nerves and tendons and veins and viscera, reaching into the remotest corners, were concentrated in me…."). And, of course, Slocum did it again and again in *Sailing Alone Around the World*. So the answer to the question, *What is seamanship?* might be to start with a checklist but be training for *oneness*.

The first thing we did after stowing our gear was to put a single reef in the mainsail. To do this we raised the sail partway up to get the weight and bulk of the gaff off the sail. We then lashed the tack of the sail to the gooseneck of the boom and then—at the other end of the boom—took up on the reef outhaul. We pulled the outhaul tight and made it fast to the cleat on the boom. I then put a lashing through the large reef cringle at the new clew and lashed it securely around the boom, being careful to slip some spare canvas between the lashing and the bunched sail. This would prevent the line from chafing against the sail. Now the sail was stretched tightly fore and aft and tied down at both the clew and tack corners. We were ready to tie the reef points. We pulled each of them through—between the foot rope and boom and not around the boom—and tied each reef point with a slippery reef knot. The sail was now ready to go. I dropped the gaff back into place, putting a single sail tie in place to keep the sail from spilling into the cockpit as we continued our preparations.

I checked the fluid levels in the engine (fuel, transmission, and lube oil) and pressed the glow plug, counting to fifteen before firing up the diesel. It started right up, and I looked over the side to be sure water was being discharged from the wet exhaust. Every two or three seconds a stream of water shot from the hole in the transom.

Spreading the chart on the settee, I plotted the course in pencil from our mooring in Diamond Pass to a buoy in Hussey Sound. Then I aligned the parallel rules on the pencil line and, being careful not to allow the rules to slip, walked the rules toward the compass

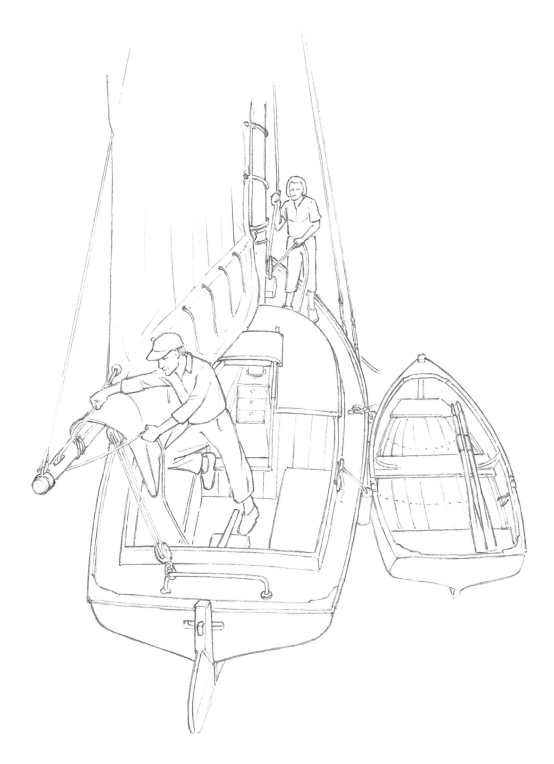

rose (using the inner, magnetic rose) and read off the course: 050°. I wrote this along the pencil line, and then drew more lines and wrote more courses, until our track for the day was complete. It would not dictate our exact course. The vagaries of the wind and waves would see to that. But it was a sketch of our course—a visual representation of how our day would unfold should we be blessed with favorable conditions and no gear failures.

I finished the notes by drawing a small, old-fashioned anchor on the east side of Inner Green Island.

Raven slipped forward to cast off the mooring. I told her I was ready, and she dropped the mooring pennant into the water. She then came aft, untied the skiff from the side cleat, and began paying out line as I pressed the boat into gear. She let out all fifty feet of line, and then she made it fast with a few swift turns around the stern cleat, followed by a single locking hitch. She took the helm from me and steadied the boat's heading directly into the northwest wind as I raised the main. Raven sheeted it in tightly as I then raised the jib. Back in the cockpit, I slacked the port jib sheet, took up on the starboard one, and Raven put the tiller over as the sails filled. I pulled the engine out of gear and let it idle for a few minutes. We were soon clipping along on a port tack, making about five knots through the water. We trimmed the sails for a beam reach and settled into our seats. A few minutes later I secured the engine. The only sound was the lapping of the waves and wind in our ears. We sat silently grinning at one another in the morning sunlight.

I always carry three items in my pants pocket: Chapstick, a cigarette lighter, and a pocketknife. And I tell anyone who will listen to do the same. The Chapstick is to guard against wind, sun, and salt. (And it's the only brand that doesn't seem to dry my lips further.) The knife is to cut lines or facilitate making lunch, and the lighter is to melt the ends of lines, build fires on a beach, or light candles or lanterns. A day on the water does not go by when I don't use each of these items at some point.

"You packin' steel?" I asked Raven.

"Yep!" She dug in her pocket and showed me her pocketknife.

The rest of the sail out to the Green Islands (Inner and Outer) was uneventful in terms of action, yet the crispness of the air, the point of sail (broad reach), and the interval of the swells was about as close an approximation to oneness with the boat and elements as one could hope for. We sneaked through Green Island Passage and then "hardened up," bringing the sheets in tight on a close (port) reach to shape a final course into the little cove on Inner Green. I went forward and untied the lashings around the little, old-fashioned anchor on the foredeck, hauled up the roughly twelve feet of chain and another fifty feet of anchor rode, and then faked it all out on deck. This way it would run fair as I let the anchor over the side. We had agreed to anchor in about fifteen feet of water, which would give us a scope ratio of almost four-to-one—plenty for a short picnic lunch and a swim if we found decent holding ground. I dropped the jib and put a sail tie around it to keep it from dragging in the water. I then stood by on the anchor as

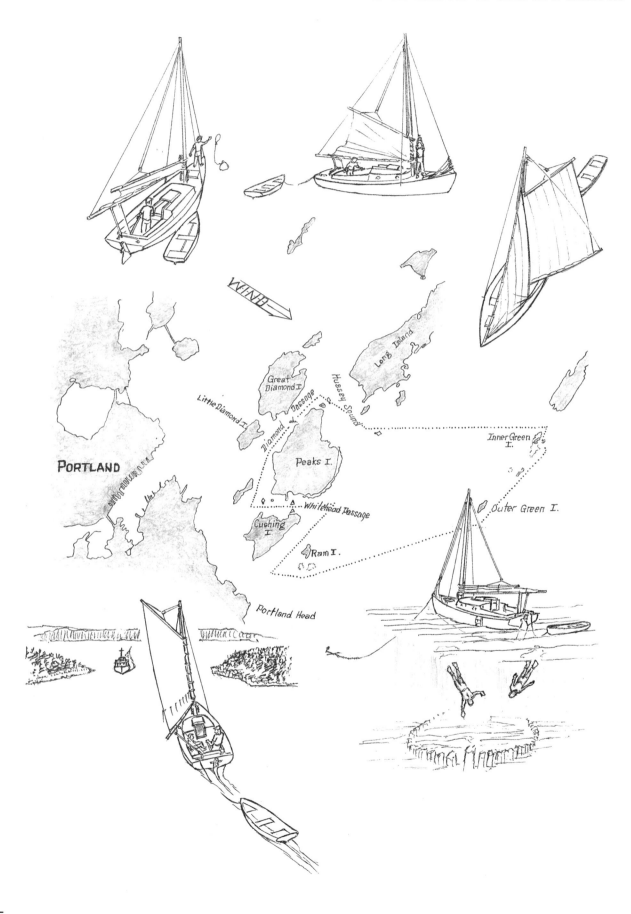

Raven nosed *Swallow* closer to the beach. I could see the bottom now and suggested she "round up"—turn directly into the wind—so that we would drift to a stop. She put the helm down, and in a few seconds the boat had come to a stop. I eased the anchor over the side and paid out chain and rode until I felt the anchor touch. We started to drift astern, so I took a single wrap on the Sampson post to set the anchor in the bottom— keeping a strain on the rode but paying it out at the same time. The line was soon at the fifty-foot mark (each fathom is marked with a small length of colored twine inserted between the strands), so I took another wrap and made a locking hitch on the post.

Meanwhile, Raven had come forward and dropped the main, a halyard (peak and throat) in each hand. We furled the sail together and were soon pulling on our wetsuits for a look at the underwater wreck we'd heard about. It was supposed to be in thirty to forty feet of water, an old fishing or lumber schooner that had taken a wrong turn or cut the Passage too close many decades ago. We splashed over the side. I checked the anchor by taking a deep breath and allowing my snorkel to fill before diving down toward the bottom. One fluke was buried deeply in the muck, a perfect set. I kicked for the surface and blew out my snorkel before starting our search.

We swam around for about twenty minutes before we found it—its frames and keel covered in growth such that we could barely discern its original shape. Its keel was ori-ented roughly in the position it must have grounded in if it drove ashore from the east, the direction of the open sea. It may have been headed for Portland with a full catch and the captain made a slight navigational error, or maybe it was ditched for more nefarious reasons. The sea would keep this secret. I again dived, kicking hard with my fins, and touched the tip of one of the ship's upwardly-pointing frames. Starfish and barnacles clung to the ancient timbers; kelp and rockweed waved in the current.

Back aboard we wriggled out of our suits, toweled dry, and spread out our lunch. The breeze was beginning to fade, so after lunch was cleared we shook out the reef in the mainsail. To do this, we simply untied the lashings on the clew and tack and pulled out the slippery reef knots along the foot of the sail. To get underway, we raised the main and hauled the anchor line back inboard until the rode was straight up and down, the anchor still somewhat set in the bottom, but we were not quite free. Raven waited until the main filled on its starboard side (a port tack), and then put the helm hard to port. I broke the anchor free of the bottom, brought the anchor aboard, and then raised the jib.

For our return sail we decided to go outside of Outer Green and shape a course for the Portland Head Light. We would then turn, just before the main shipping channel that passes the light, and work our way between the islands through Whitehead Passage, a narrow channel that separates Peaks from Cushing islands. The wind would be blowing dead against us in the Pass, but we had the tide with us, and the wind was still fresh enough to allow us good speed through the water.

An hour later we were just turning toward Whitehead Passage when we noticed another vessel about to enter the Pass from the other end. It appeared to be one of the moderately-sized ferries that serve the islands of Casco Bay. Now, I've been sailing long enough to know that Murphy's Law dictates that we would meet one another at the exact narrowest part of the channel, a place where a ledge makes out from Cushing Island, marked by a green daymark on a metal pole, and a red nun opposite marking another shallow spot. This little squeeze is barely fifty yards wide. We could, Raven and I, technically assert our right of way. We were a sailing vessel, and this ferry was a power-driven vessel. But there is the letter of the law, and then there's the Law of Tonnage and the common courtesy of making room for a vessel that is working on the water.

The so-called "Rules of the Nautical Road," also called the COLREGS, short for "Collision Regulations," are a collection of laws that govern the behavior of ships at sea as they come into close contact with one another. They dictate proper light displays onboard ship, delineate safe maneuvers and appropriate sound signals for vessels crossing or passing one another, and proscribe the Rules' applicability around the country's territorial waters and international high seas. They are terribly confusing at first. There are multiple pages of light displays showing the various lights for fishing vessels, mine-sweeping operations, dredging, and sailing and commercial vessels. There are countless scenarios describing "if this, then that" between two vessels. But after reading through them a few times, patterns begin to emerge. They make sense. Avoid, if at all possible, a turn to port, for example. If both vessels react to close-quarters situations in this way, they turn away from one another. Similarly, a vessel on the port side of another vessel must give way to the starboard (or "stand-on") vessel, and you are reminded of this fact if you're aboard the give-way vessel because you can see the red running light of the stand-on vessel. And he can see your green light. (Red = stop! Green = go!) It's worth reading the Rules over a few times and then keeping a copy handy in the nav kit for quick reference. (My *Pocket Rules* measures only five by three inches; I keep it in the same Tupperware box as the parallel rules and dividers.)

The ferry soon departed the Pass and continued on its course down Bay. We came about and were soon tacking our way into Whitehead Passage, swept along by the favorable tide. I handled the jib sheets as Raven sat at the tiller, edging *Swallow* closely against ledges on one side and then the other, getting as close as she dared before saying "Ready about!" and putting the tiller down.

The sun was still high in the sky when we approached our mooring in Diamond Pass. I picked up the pennant on the first try—dousing the sails at the last moment in a fashion that would make Herreshoff's fictional captains, Goddard and Coridon, proud. We had used the engine just twenty minutes today—just long enough to allow it to stretch its legs and come up to temperature. I took my turn at the oars that afternoon, allowing Raven the chance to relax in the stern sheets as I looked back at *Swallow,* bobbing at her mooring like a gull.

It had been a perfect day, a sublime combination of mild adventure in a beautiful setting on a summer's day.

In the Introduction to this book I challenged the reader to not get bogged down in the minutia of learning to sail—to learn by reading, but mostly to learn by doing, to go for it.

Here, then, is your chance.

ANNOTATED BIBLIOGRAPHY

T he following books were used in the research and writing of *The Complete Guide to Sailing & Seamanship*. They are not an exhaustive list of a complete maritime library, but they are books I keep close at hand for constant reference when considering a sailing voyage, whether for an afternoon, a few days, or a week or more. Even the fiction selections I find useful and inspiring.

American Merchant Seaman's Manual, Fifth Edition, edited by Felix M. Cornell and Allan C. Hoffman, Cornell Maritime Press, copyright 1964. The *Manual* is full of wonderful information on all manner of seamanship basics. Most of it is useful mainly to the deep-sea merchant seaman, but it's brimming with good seamanship skills that are ubiquitous in their scope. It's still standard reading at maritime academies. Now in its seventh edition, a new copy costs over $100, but I bought my copy (fifth edition) for $.25 at a junk shop in Rockland, Maine. Most of the information will never be dated, and the older copies make more interesting reading anyway.

American Practical Navigator, by Nathaniel Bowditch, National Image and Mapping Agency (NIMA)/Paradise Cay Publications, copyright 2011. *Bowditch*, as this book is invariably referred to, changed the world of navigation when it was first published in 1802. It's been continuously updated and remains the definitive volume on navigating a vessel of any size.

American Small Sailing Craft, by Howard Chapelle, W.W. Norton & Co., copyright 1951. Howard Chapelle devoted his life to documenting the small craft and sailing ships that were quickly disappearing in the middle of the 20th century. This book is a treasure trove of boat design and how local conditions and particular uses inform their function. As a result, it's also an elegy to America's working-sail heritage.

The Arts of the Sailor, by Hervey Garrett Smith, Dover Publications, copyright 1990. This little book offers excellent illustrations on making simple and decorative knots, handling line in coils, and making a variety of splices. It is a beautiful book with clear illustrations. It offers none of the dizzying complexity of a tome like *The Ashley Book of Knots*, which is its charm and value.

Boatowner's Mechanical and Electrical Manual, Third Edition, by Nigel Calder, International Marine/McGraw Hill, copyright 2005. This book explains every little detail on managing engines, systems, and electronics on a small boat. It is truly indispensible for the owner of a boat with even the simplest of systems and electronics.

The Captain, by Jan de Hartog, Atheneum, copyright 1966. The protagonist Martinus Harinxma begins the book as a newly-minted captain in the British Navy early in World War II. He feels woefully unprepared and soon discovers that his skills as a seaman are less important than his capacity as a leader. For someone new to operating one's own boat, this book provides a fine view of the effectiveness of humility and compassion, but also boldness and action, in a position of authority.

The Compleat Cruiser: The Art, Practice and Enjoyment of Boating, by L. Francis Herreshoff, Seafarer Books, copyright 1991 (originally published in 1956).

The Craft of Sail: A Primer of Sailing, by Jan Adkins, Walker and Company, copyright 1973. I first used this book to really learn how a sailing rig interacts with a hull and the wind and waves to go in a desired direction. The drawings are both simple and beautiful but also highly instructive.

Endurance, by Alfred Lansing, McGraw-Hill Book Co., Inc., copyright 1959. A run of recent books have revisited Ernest Shackleton's legendary exploits of 1915, but each lacks the force of this original tale, published while many of the crewmembers of the ill-fated Antarctic expedition were still alive. The tale is exceptionally told, and the sea drama—the crossing of the Drake Passage in tiny boats—offers wonderful insight into one of history's most incredible boat journeys.

Eric Sloane's Weather Book, by Eric Sloane, Dover Publications, copyright 2005. Sloane's black-and-white illustrations, combined with his practical advice on observing weather phenomena, make this book a fine introduction to understanding basic weather. It is not written from a sailor's perspective, but it's certainly a useful primer wherever your outdoor adventures take you.

Gipsy Moth Circles the World, by Sir Francis Chichester, copyright 1967. Chichester, an accomplished RAF pilot who first set several solo flight records, would be the first to circumnavigate the earth alone with only a single stopover. That he was dying slowly of cancer—and his advanced age of almost seventy years old—was likely the reason he wasn't the first to solo nonstop.

The Grey Seas Under: The Perilous Rescue Missions of a North Atlantic Salvage Tug, by Farley Mowat, Little, Brown and Company, copyright 1958. Mowat describes the travails of the crew of *Foundation Franklin* throughout their career as commercial salvors in the North Atlantic following the end of World War II. The seamanship exploits are mind-boggling and the book might well inspire the reader to seriously consider running away to sea to become a salvor. The risks are great, but the rewards are potentially enormous.

How to Abandon Ship, by Phil Richards and John J. Banigan, Cornell Maritime Press, copyright 1988. This is the finest book of its kind—full of disasters from which you can glean solid seamanship skills. The writing is so spare and concise, the images so crisp and brilliant, that you find yourself wondering if it qualifies as poetry.

Introduction to Nautical Science, by Carl Chase, W.W. Norton and Co., copyright 1990. Chase has a way of explaining navigational basics, from lines of position to sun lines, in a spare style that does not get cluttered in too much detail. The book also includes sections (and diagrams) on docking and sailhandling, making it a fine beginner's volume for navigating and sailing larger vessels.

Moitessier: A Sailing Legend, by Jean-Michel Barrault, Sheridan House, copyright 2005. Bernard Moitessier, like his English counterpart Francis Chichester, was truly a sailing legend. His book *The Long Way*, an account of participating in the Golden Globe Race, is Moitessier's finest literary effort. He is revered as a bit of a mystic amongst certain types of sailors, not least because of his eschewing the race but also for his poetic rambles: "I watch this fantastic sea, breathe in its spray, and feel blossoming here in the wind and space something that needs the immensity of the universe to come to fruition."

N by E, by Rockwell Kent, Brewer & Warren, copyright 1930. Rockwell Kent was a rascal who had a penchant for slipping away from his various wives without a moment's notice to sail to far-off lands. He sailed to Cape Horn, Greenland, Alaska, and up and down the U.S. East Coast, on boats large and small. And he was a wonderfully lucid writer. Kent's books have the added advantage of being illustrated by his bold black-and-white woodcuts. *N by E* tells the story of his adventure sailing from New York to Greenland and how his little boat, *Direction*, was wrecked in the process. It's a thrilling tale of adventure.

The Nature of Boats: Insights and Esoterica for the Nautically Obsessed, by Dave Gerr, International Marine, copyright 1992. Dave Gerr is a genius, and this book reflects that fact. It's full of nautical data, but it's written in such a chirpy, fun style, almost like the children's book *How Things Work*, that it's a pleasure to dig into some of the harder topics, such as horsepower ("The Care and Feeding of a Power Plant"), torque ("Let's Talk Torquey"), and marine electronics ("Keeping Electrons on the Straight and Narrow").

Ocean Navigator's Pocket Rules of the Road, edited by Charlie Wing, Navigator Publishing, copyright 1998. *The Nautical Rules of the Road* are published in a variety of forms. I prefer this volume because it is tiny and can be stowed on a nav desk or tucked into a small navigational kit for quick reference. The Rules can be confusing, but they are worth skimming somewhat regularly so that you don't get in trouble on congested waters, especially with commercial vessels.

Oceanography and Seamanship, Second Edition, by William G. Van Dorn, Cornell Maritime Press, copyright 1993. The author, a physical oceanographer, provides a vast array of information, from meteorology to ocean currents, weather forecasting to wave predictions and heavy weather seamanship. This is a massive text for the truly determined boatowner.

Radar For Mariners, by David Burch, McGraw-Hill, copyright 2004. As discussed in the chapter on navigation, radar is more of a large-vessel tool than one intended for day-sailers. However, should you equip your vessel with radar, learn to use it. This simple book offers the basics—and more.

Sailing Alone Around the World, by Joshua Slocum, Blue Ribbon Books, The Century Co., copyright 1900. This first edition includes drawings by Thomas Fogarty and George Varian, a feature not all the later editions include. (The drawings were taken from sketches by Slocum himself.) Whatever edition, however, the book is a beautiful story about a man communing with the sea and his little vessel. His self-reliance (and self-deprecation) is a true inspiration for any aspiring sailor. He lives for the proposition that enjoying the sea requires very little in terms of gear, just a good attitude and a lot of pluck.

Seraffyn's Mediterranean Adventure, by Lin and Larry Pardey, Sheridan House, copyright 1991. The Pardeys have been sailing full time for more than forty years and have published more than ten books on the subject, including their popular *Storm Tactics Handbook*. They espouse a kind of seamanship that eschews modern contrivances and relies instead on self-reliance and common sense. None of their boats has had an engine. Their web site is also full of sailing wisdom and wonderful sea stories (www. landlpardey.com).

Shop Class as Soulcraft: An Inquiry Into the Value of Work, by Matthew B. Crawford, The Penguin Press, copyright 2009. This book has nothing to do with the sea, but it espouses a worthy view of the value of working with one's hands, something that every sailor finds necessary at some point in his or her sailing life.

Swallows & Amazons, Sixth Edition, by Arthur Ransome, David R. Godine, Publisher, Inc., copyright 1993. This is a book included for parents or grandparents of young children. Originally published in 1930, this story was likely responsible for sending many young adults to sea in the 1930s and '40s. The story is simply about a group of children spending a summer sailing their little sailboat on a lake. But it projects a sense of wonder at the unique language and adventure of the sea that makes the story not just a good sea yarn but also one that can serve today's helicopter parents to encourage their children to explore nature and to take reasonable risks. This old tale (which is somewhat dated in its language and style) may serve as a welcome antidote for our time when "nature deficit disorder" is creating a sense of fear of, and sense of apartness from, the out-of-doors and the natural environment as a whole. Letting children explore on their own (with safe parameters) nourishes creative play and develops the willpower of children. Exploring the natural world from the cockpit of a small boat is a perfect way to do this.

Two Years Before the Mast, by Richard Henry Dana, Henry Altimus, copyright 1895 (originally published 1840). The author went to sea to cure his eye trouble and general malaise, but he ended up writing the most unique and enduring true-life sea story of the era.

A Voyage for Madmen, by Peter Nichols, HarperCollins, copyright 2001. This book documents the Golden Globe around-the-world race, featuring Moitessier and Knox-Johnston and the raving Donald Crowhurst, who likely committed suicide at sea following a mass deception of his progress in the race. Nichols is an accomplished, single-handed sailor himself, making the book as much a treatise on seamanship as it is about the challenges of the human spirit in isolation and under stress.

Wanderer, by Sterling Hayden, Sheridan House, copyright 1998 (originally 1963). Sterling Hayden may not have had the most integrity when it came to dealing with his shoreside responsibilities, but he cannot be matched for seagoing exuberance.

Wanderer tells the story of his escape from the law in California to the high seas and tropical isles of the South Pacific.

"The Wreck of the Hesperus," by Henry Wadsworth Longfellow. First published in *Ballads and Other Poems* in 1842.

Youth, by Joseph Conrad, Doubleday, Page & Co., copyright 1925. This novella first inspired me to love the sea. Written in an exuberant voice, it's vintage Conrad, growling about the romance of youth afflicted with a love of the sea with both affection and wisdom. No nautical library is complete without a smattering of Joseph Conrad.

ACKNOWLEDGEMENTS

This book is the result of twenty years of sailing adventures, from my green-hand days as a student at Sea Semester in Woods Hole, Mass., aboard *Westward* and *Corwith Cramer*, to sailing in open boats at the Chewonki Foundation in Wiscasset, Maine, to Ray Williamson's Camden windjammer fleet, affectionately and somewhat notoriously known as the "Green Boats," to *Ocean Navigator*'s training schooner *Ocean Star*, and later as co-owner of Portland Schooner Co. in Portland, Maine. Along the way I have also been privileged to perform numerous yacht deliveries and sail alongside many wonderful people who deserve praise for their patience, seamanship expertise, and good humor: Greg Walsh, Michael Carr, Virginia Wagner, David Jones, Shaye McGann, Jess Burton, Ponch Membreño, Carlos Cantone, Ray Williamson, Steve Pixley, Jeff Lovejoy, Troy Scott, Hannah Sieben, John Snyder, Chuck Husick, Scott Reischmann, and Michelle Thresher, to name a few.

This book was also supported behind the scenes by numerous others, in particular my mentor and good friend Sam Manning. Special thanks: Jenn McCartney and Tony Lyons of Skyhorse; Tim Queeney, my editor and distinguished colleague at *Ocean Navigator* Magazine, where parts of this book first appeared in somewhat different form; Matt Hume, fellow *Bowditch* enthusiast, for his careful review of the text; my mother, Sandra Braden, for early edits; my brother Trevor Braden for always being up for a sea voyage; and my wonderful wife, Leah Day, and our four adventuresome children, Oakley, Raven, Jonah, and Finn—the best shipmates of all.

INDEX

Page numbers in parentheses indicate pages in which the word in question is in an illustration or the acknowledgments.

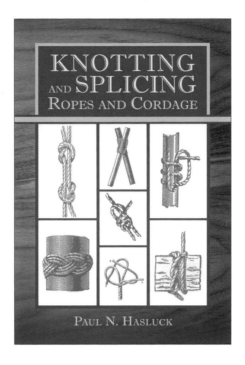

Knotting and Splicing Ropes and Cordage

by Paul N. Hasluck

When it comes to explaining crafters' tools and techniques, craftsman Paul N. Hasluck is a true master. In *Knotting and Splicing Ropes and Cordage*, Hasluck covers everything, from the basics of rope formation to tying useful knots, splicing rope, working cordage, tying fancy knots, using different ties and lashings, and more—all among more than two hundred intricate illustrations. Great for sailors, scouts, climbers, cavers, rescue workers, or anyone who is simply interested in learning the skills behind knotting and splicing, this classic work holds the very foundation of the art.

$12.95 Paperback • ISBN 978-1-61608-678-7

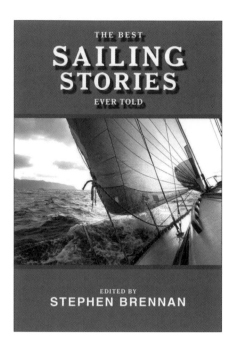

The Best Sailing Stories Ever Told

Edited by Stephen Brennan

For thousands of years, we have set out sailing for all kinds of reasons—for battle, for infinite wealth, for the excitement of exploring the unknown, and for escape from the mundane. We have always had a primal relationship with the sea—even those who have never been to sea remain fascinated by the seafaring life and tales of salty adventure. Now in a brand-new series collection, *The Best Sailing Stories Ever Told* brings together such diverse authors as Charles Dickens, Jack London, John Masefield, Stephen Crane, Herman Melville, and dozens more. Many of the writers featured here are instantly recognizable and have achieved deserved fame; others who are lesser known and rarely featured in print take their rightful place on the shelves of sailing literature.

Lovers of the seascape will certainly get their fill with this shimmering sample of sea tales that range from the ancient epic and biblical stories to contemporary captains of literature. Whether you're itching for a sailor's peaceful life at sea, his epic conquest of the azure blue, or his own private descent into madness, this collection touches on the many aspects of life at sea. Each story is illustrated with black-and-white line art that makes this book a true classic. Even if you are enjoying *The Best Sailing Stories Ever Told* from the warm, dry comfort of your own living room, you are sure to be inspired by the colorful and stirring stories in this timeless collection.

$12.95 Paperback • ISBN 978-1-61608-219-2

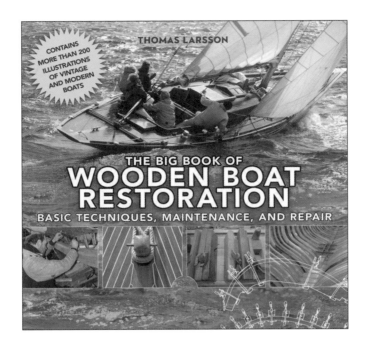

The Big Book of Wooden Boat Restoration
Basic Techniques, Maintenance, and Repair
by Thomas Larsson

The Big Book of Wooden Boat Restoration is the perfect introduction or reference guide for wooden boat lovers both experienced and new. Author Thomas Larsson, one of Sweden's most experienced and premier wooden boat restorers, has created a restoration book accessible to new hobbyists and longtime boat lovers alike.

This book contains chapters on boat care, including winter maintenance, racing, finishing, and stripping. You will also find current information on boat building, gluing, and tools. Chapters also describe the detailed repair of wooden boats—everything from plug-accession and bonding to changing socks and bottom engine installation.

$24.95 Hardcover • ISBN 978-1-62087-051-8

Navigation Rules
International: Inland

by the U.S. Coast Guard

For anyone who owns a boat this is a neccessary handbook. Included are all of the official government rules and regulations that must be followed by anyone out on the water. This book will prepare you for head-on situations, avoiding collisions, and using distress signals, and will inform you of all the up-to-date water regulations. Whether you're in a jam or just relaxing at sea, *Navigation Rules* will teach and prepare you for anything and everything you may encounter while on your boat.

$9.95 Paperback • ISBN 978-1-61608-243-7

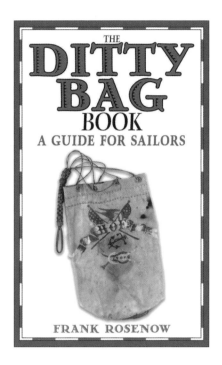

The Ditty Bag Book
A Guide for Sailors

by Frank Rosenow

Sailors have used ditty bags to carry sewing equipment, toiletries, and other small items for centuries, and now *The Ditty Bag Book* teaches modern-day sailors the art form of hand-making ditty bags to use on their own seaward travels. Master sailor Frank Rosenow provides complete, step-by-step instructions in the making of a ditty bag—from cutting material to size to decorative touches—and emphasizes the proper maintenance of rigging and sails using the items stowed in the ditty bag.

Included in this handy, portable guide is additional information about the essential tools any sailor should have aboard ship, such as a clasp knife, a hand-seaming palm, beeswax, and a serving mallet. Rosenow also offers an array of advice on repairing sails, splicing, palm-and-needle whippings, chafing gear, and much more! Complete with hand drawings by the author, *The Ditty Bag Book* is essential for any modern-day sailor.

$14.95 Paperback • ISBN 978-1-61608-187-4

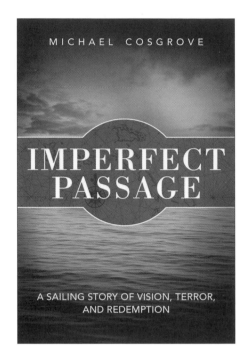

Imperfect Passage
A Sailing Story of Vision, Terror, and Redemption
by Michael Cosgrove

www.imperfectpassage.com

Michael Cosgrove had a beautiful family, a successful career, and a lovely Southern California home overlooking the Pacific Ocean. At the age of sixty, he decided to leave all that behind to sail around the world.

In spite of his romanticized vision of rugged individualism and the salty tales he'd have to share with his grandchildren, Cosgrove quickly realizes that sailing around the world isn't going to be as easy as he'd imagined. From a psychotic crewmate, sleep deprivation, and mental breakdowns, to stormy weather and hallucinations, Cosgrove rides the waves, holding on as best he can to his dream of "doing something grand." Alone, and thousands of miles away from everyone and everything he loves, he is forced to ask himself one question: What in God's name am I doing here?

$24.95 Hardcover • ISBN 978-1-61608-728-9

NOTES

NOTES

NOTES

NOTES

NOTES

NOTES